Power in
PRAYER

DAVID A. CHRISTENSEN

D1081762

CFI
An Imprint of Cedar Fort, Inc.
Springville, Utah

ISBN 13: 978-1-4621-1287-6

Published by CFI, an imprint of Cedar Fort, Inc.
2373 W. 700 S., Springville, UT 84663
Distributed by Cedar Fort, Inc., www.cedarfort.com

LIBRARY OF CONGRESS CATALOGING-IN-PUBLICATION DATA

Christensen, David A., 1949- author.
Power in prayer : 31 teachings to strengthen our connection with heaven / David A. Christensen.
    pages cm
ISBN 978-1-4621-1287-6
1. Prayer--Church of Jesus Christ of Latter-day Saints. 2. Mormons--Religious life. I. Title.
BX8656.C4935 2013
248.3'2--dc23
                                2013034171

Cover design by Shawnda T. Craig
Cover design © 2014 Lyle Mortimer
Edited and typeset by Emily S. Chambers

Printed in the United States of America

10 9 8 7 6 5 4 3 2 1

Printed on acid-free paper

Contents

CONTENTS

Introduction

I have always had tender feelings about prayer. One of the first things I learned to do as a toddler was to fold my arms, bow my head, and say the words "Heavenly Father," "Jesus Christ," and "amen." Two or three times a day we prayed as a family. It was the Vaughn and Irene Christensen family tradition to kneel beside our chairs at breakfast, and again at dinner to have family prayer before we ate. As a baby, too small to kneel, I was permitted to sit in my high chair and was taught to fold my arms and bow my head for as long as my attention span would allow. No doubt I would have lost focus in a few seconds and spent the rest of the prayer as an observer—watching Dad, Mom, Carole, Janice, Ken, Steve, and Marv kneeling and talking to Heavenly Father. I no doubt waited with anticipation for the person acting voice to say "amen" so that I could echo the ending of that prayer with my own "amen." As a right of passage, when we moved to the "big people chairs," we would join in the kneeling process, and, when ready, we'd say a simple prayer.

Lunchtime included a blessing on the food, and individual bedtime prayers were a constant in our home. We prayed before scripture time, at family home evening, and whenever we learned someone in the family or ward needed a special blessing. Whenever a toy was lost, we were encouraged to kneel and ask Heavenly Father to help us remember where we put it or to help us find it. When we got scared, we prayed for peace and protection. If we argued with a sibling, we were invited to go to our bedroom, work it out, and ask Heavenly Father to help us make amends.

Prayer was never a forced practice but rather a part of life. I have been grateful for the blessing of having prayer be such a fundamental and indispensable part of living. I believe I can say that in nearly six decades of life on earth, I have never gone to bed without kneeling first for at least a cursory acknowledgment to Heavenly Father in prayer. No doubt there were times as a child when I fell asleep watching TV or riding home in a car or such, when I was in dreamland and nothing could bring me back to this sphere. But that didn't happen very often. I estimate that I've knelt by my bed and prayed no less than twenty thousand times.

My point is simply that prayer—the act of acknowledging God as Father in Heaven and doing it in the name of Jesus Christ—is as familiar to me as putting on my clothes or eating a meal. I have no doubt I've prayed with more consistency than even brushing my teeth. And that single act has had an important impact on my life.

Have my prayers been too short and included vain repetitions? Yes. Have I violated the principles considered for "good prayers" or "worthy communication" with God in Heaven? Yes. Could I have done a better job in communicating to Father in Heaven in morning prayer to open my day? Absolutely!

All those prayers—private, family, public, formal, and informal—have given me a testimony that prayer is important. One of Jehovah's first admonitions or commandments to Adam and Eve, when they were cast out of the Garden of Eden, was to "call upon the name of the Lord forevermore" (Moses 5:8).

I have a testimony of prayer. It is my desire to share that testimony with you in hopes that your own life will be blessed by self-examination and improving your prayer life. I have learned important principles about prayer and have found that latter-day prophets, seers, and revelators have counseled us with hundreds of things we can do to improve our prayer lives and to maintain a relationship with Heavenly Father. This improvement will, in turn, give us so many other blessings and opportunities.

Some of what I have learned, I will share throughout the chapters of this short book. There are a few fundamental principles I want to share now. They are basic and essential to the processes of a strong prayer life. I hope the following truths will create a context in helping you take away something of value in each of the chapters that follow.

Principle 1: Connection with Heaven Takes Work

The first principle is found in a symbol that came to me many years ago. The symbol is two links of chain bound together.

To me this symbolizes the importance of prayer as a connection between me and my Father in Heaven. I put the two-link piece of chain on my key ring. Having it there provided a reminder of the important things I had learned about prayer. It later became a fundamental centerpiece in my ministry as a bishop, stake president, mission president, and MTC president. As a professor teaching missionary preparation at BYU–Idaho, I would begin the semester with a lesson about the importance of creating and maintaining an excellent prayer life. The symbol of the chain link laced together every lesson with the question "How is your prayer life?" On the last day of class, I would give each my students a chain link to put on their key ring, (or some strategic place on their backpack or purse). Naturally, each member of my family received the symbol in a family home evening. Over the years, I gave one to each of the youth in the wards where I've served. The chain link became a symbol I shared with 563 missionaries in Chile and approximately 2,000 missionaries who passed through the MTC in Guatemala. I project that well over ten thousand two-link chain pieces have passed through my hands to others as a simple token or reminder of the profound importance of prayer.

No doubt the local hardware stores in Arizona, Michigan, Florida, and especially in Idaho, Chile, and Guatemala have wondered what I do with all that chain. When I taught at BYU–Idaho, I would see freshly returned missionaries who had been students in my mission preparation classes. The first thing they did was pull their key ring from their pocket and show me their chain link. With a smile, they would say, "I still have it and my prayer life has never been better."

My purpose in sharing this, is that the symbol of the chain link, or one like it, can become a powerful reminder of the importance of being *connected* to Father in Heaven through prayer.

I am told by a professional in metallurgy that "properly implemented, a welding point is stronger than the base metal that it connects; the base metal will break before the weld." The place of the weld is stronger than the metal it is holding together. The links that are welded together become very powerful. In the same way, the process of correctly implementing a connection with Heavenly Father becomes a powerful source in our lives. The Bible Dictionary states, "Prayer is a form of work and is an appointed means for obtaining the highest of all blessings." It also teaches that "blessings require some work or effort on our part before we can obtain them." We must work to be connected to Heavenly Father. We must consider proper implementation to keep us inseparably connected to the power of heaven.

The simple symbol of a chain link on my key ring has helped me and hundreds of others remember the importance of working toward and staying connected to Heavenly Father through His Son Jesus Christ.

Principle 2: One's Spiritual Life Is No Greater than the Quality of One's Prayer Life

I have learned that a person's prayer life is a barometer of the quality of his or her spirituality. If there is a consistent effort to stay connected to the Lord, then clearly the life and action of that person is more directed and centered on Jesus Christ. A person's spirituality will never be greater than the quality of his or her prayer life.

I have also learned that besides the *quality* of prayer life, the *quantity* of prayers uttered daily impacts how connected a person is with heaven.

We have all heard returned missionaries comment on their mission being the greatest two years of their lives. Much of that is because they are so connected to heaven. I have asked hundreds of missionaries how many times they prayed each day. Some say more than twenty times and many say they were praying all the time. Think about it—praying formally with investigators, in district meetings, at zone conferences, in the homes of members, and at church. They have personal prayers and companionship prayers several times each day. They then pray many informal prayers uttered in their mind or heart on behalf of a companion during his teaching, on the doorstep, thinking about the needs of some investigator, or that fervent prayer in the heart as they begin a street contact. In short, their prayer life is at a lifetime high.

Then I've asked the same returned missionaries about their daily prayer life after they returned home.

For some, the answers are "maybe a couple of times each day" or "I just forget." When they leave their missions, the number of times they pray each day is reduced by 90 percent or more. Oftentimes in either one-on-one interviews or while engaging in discussion when visiting elders quorum meetings, they would share more personal answers like "honestly, I have to struggle to have one meaningful prayer a day" or "it's hard to have prayer when so much is going on in the apartment with roommates."

The quantity of prayers offered daily does matter in a healthy prayer life and focused connection with heaven. It may be that in regular life, it is not expected to spend the same amount of time praying as when serving a mission. However, a mix of formal and informal personal prayers along with public prayers in quantity is important.

Principle 3: The Quantity of Informal Prayer Is an Effective Indicator of a Prayer Life

I think it's generally understood that formal personal prayers are offered two or three times a day. Alma counseled his son Helaman to "counsel with the Lord in all [our] doings, and he will direct thee for good, yea, when thou liest down at night unto the Lord, that he may watch over you in your sleep; and when thou risest in the morning let thy heart be full of thanks unto God" (Alma 37:37).

But let's talk about the part of his counsel when he says, "Cry unto God for all thy support; yea, let all thy doings be unto the Lord, and whithersoever thou goest let it be in the Lord; yea, let all thy thoughts be directed unto the Lord; yea, let the affections of thy heart be placed upon the Lord forever" (Alma 37:36).

What does "let all thy doings be unto the Lord" look like? How can one really have a prayer life that looks like "whithersoever thou goest let it be in the Lord" and to "let it be directed unto the Lord" and to have "the affections of our hearts placed upon the Lord forever"? It sounds as though, except for our hours of sleep, we are counseled to be completely and totally focused on the Lord. One way to do that is to have lots of informal prayers. Talking and walking with the Lord continually.

We may find ourselves uttering silent prayers like "Thank you Heavenly Father for the sunrise—it's so beautiful." or "Heavenly Father, help me to be calm—Bobby just threw the cat into the dryer!" Perhaps it's an utterance like "Father, help me to have wisdom and judgment in this business decision regarding whether to accept a business contract with this entity" or "Father, I haven't studied as well as I should have for this test; however, please help me with the power to reason based upon what I have learned." Maybe a young man walking in a shopping mall may silently plea "Father, here she comes; in the name of Jesus Christ, bless me to keep my mind and eyes where they should be in order to honor thee."

It seems that mixing in scores of silent informal prayers to heaven along with two or three formal prayers each day will help in keeping us connected to Heaven and focused on God and Christ.

Principle 4: Prayer Is the First to Go

For some reason, prayer is often the first thing to go. Somehow, the busy things of the world crowd out the important, critical elements that keep us connected to God, Christ, and the Holy Ghost.

I don't know what your study habits are or how much time you can dedicate to reading scriptures, and other books like this. I have written in hope to give you short thoughts based upon the teachings of a prophet, seer, and revelator.

Perhaps you could read one each day and commit to apply it in your life. A time periodically dedicated to studying about prayer and then examining our prayer lives, can bless us and keep us connected to the powers of heaven.

I look forward to being with you on this study of the subject of prayer.

1

No Appointment Necessary

"I have learned from countless personal experiences that great is the power of prayer. No earthly authority can separate us from direct access to our Creator. There can never be a mechanical or electronic failure when we pray. There is no limit on the number of times or how long we can pray each day. There is no quota of how many needs we wish to pray for in each prayer. We do not need to go through secretaries or make an appointment to reach the throne of grace. He is reachable at any time and any place" (James E. Faust, "The Lifeline of Prayer," *Ensign*, May 2002)

Aren't we pleased to understand the great truth that through the medium of prayer we can access our Father in Heaven through His Son Jesus Christ at anytime? Through infinite means that our finite minds have difficulty comprehending, Heavenly Father, as an omnipotent and omniscient being, listens to every prayer uttered and directed to Him in the name of His Son Jesus Christ. He has capacity to hear and answer the simplest prayer of a child seeking to know where to find a lost toy; or the pleading prayer of a broken-hearted mother for her son who has violated his covenants; or the prayer of gratitude expressed by a missionary far away from home for an unexpected tender mercy. Each prayer is heard, registered, and answered. We are blessed by that understanding.

Not long ago, I needed some information regarding a project I was working on. I needed to talk to the president of a large company taking no more than three minutes of his time to inquire about his perspective and experience with a certain issue. I first had to make contact with his secretary and schedule a time. I finally got a hold of his secretary who indicated she would talk with him and identify a time we could discuss the matter. Two days passed, and when I called again his secretary apologized saying that she had not been able to find even a minute to discuss my need with him. She asked for an extension of time. Another day passed and I finally received an answer indicating I could have a phone appointment two weeks later as he was traveling and occupied by a large transaction his company was negotiating. This was certainly a small item for him—yet an important one to me. I placed the information in my electronic calendar and arranged my own schedule to be available when he called. The day and hour arrived. I waited for the call, but it never came. The following morning, I called his secretary and again she apologized for her boss. Unexpected challenges arose in his day, and he was unable to call but promised to be available the following week. Another time was set up. But a few days later (about three days before the appointed time) I came from a meeting where

I had turned off my cell phone to find a message on my voicemail from the secretary that said "Mr. _____ has time to talk right now, but he will need to leave in twenty minutes. If you get this message before 2:00 p.m., call me and I will put you in contact with him." I looked at my watch. It was 2:20 p.m. I will spare the details of my frustration and the additional days that passed before I finally made connection with him.

Students may experience similar frustration. As a professor on a university campus, I know students sometimes find the class they need gets full before they have a chance to register. A common procedure is to go directly to the professor to try to get a seat or to at least get on a waiting list. A teacher can get a hundred or more emails, telephone voicemail messages, and notes slipped under their office door from anxious students who are seeking to join a class. The students expend great and creative efforts for an answer or an indication of some level of hope. Professors do the best they can but no doubt many students have gone away without any attention or response.

Another example: A few years ago, in the month of December, my aging but healthy dad had severe shoulder pain. He sought medical help and perspective. The earliest he could get an appointment for testing was in late February. The appointment was set and a painful wait ensued. Dad died in early January without ever having been seen by the specialist.

When we need to connect with God our Father, we can simply pray. We can discuss our need without arranging or clearing calendars to correlate with His. What a wonderful blessing and relief!

Prayer Self-Examination

1. Think back to your prayers in the past twenty-four hours. Did you pray this morning? How about last night? Yesterday morning? Throughout the day?
2. Do you have a specific habit and routine for your formal personal prayer time?
3. Have you identified a place where you can have peace, quiet, and a designated time to connect with Heavenly Father?

Scriptures for Consideration and Marking

3 Nephi 13:6	Job 13:22
Matthew 6:6	Jeremiah 29:12
Alma 34: 18–28	1 Nephi 18:3

A Parting Thought

While we don't need to set an appointment to access Heavenly Father, it is often good to set an appointment for ourselves to talk to Him. If we don't, busy schedules and tired bodies can get in the way and crowd out the vital act of prayer. I have found that my own connection with Heavenly Father in formal personal prayer is best when I have a routine: a time, place, and environment—"an appointment" for myself to work at communion and connection with Him. Perhaps a traditional bedside prayer is most common, but another place in the home, the backyard, or even the automobile may be a quiet and suitable place. The time is up to you—He will be waiting.

2

You Are Trusted!

"What do you do when you have prepared carefully, have prayed fervently, have waited a reasonable time for a response, and still do not feel an answer? You may want to express thanks when that occurs, for it is an evidence of His trust. When you are living worthily and your choice is consistent with the Savior's teachings and you need to act, proceed with trust. As you are sensitive to the promptings of the Spirit, one of two things will certainly occur at the appropriate time: either the stupor of thought will come, indicating an improper choice, or the peace or the burning in the bosom will be felt, confirming that your choice was correct. When you are living righteously and are acting with trust, God will not let you proceed too far without a warning impression if you have made the wrong decision." (Richard G. Scott, "Using the Supernal Gift of Prayer," *Ensign*, May 2007, 10)

N o one receives quick answers to every prayer uttered. It is normal to pray, hoping to find an answer to our heartfelt needs, only to feel no clear answer. Have you ever considered what Elder Scott teaches—that we should express gratitude when that occurs? Could it really be that no answer is really evidence that Father trusts us to make a decision on our own?

I honestly had never considered that possibility. As I think about it however, that is a concept easy to understand. In my experience as a mission president in South America, I found a few missionaries who wanted to be guided in nearly every decision regarding teaching and sharing the gospel. They would call their zone leader or me for instructions on nearly everything. And then a few other missionaries did things their own way, sometimes even against my counsel. However, many obediently acted under the influence of the Holy Ghost. I came to trust those missionaries. I knew wherever I sent them and in whatever circumstance, I could count on them. I didn't have to spend time or energy worrying about them.

What a blessing those missionaries were for a mission president with many concerns. But it's possible for that trust to be misinterpreted.

For example, one such extraordinary elder wrote to me a few years after we both returned from our service. He asked, "President, I have always wondered why I was never given the opportunity to serve as a zone leader or other responsible position in the mission. Can you just comment on that?" Wow, was I flabbergasted. This excellent missionary had carried an uneasiness in his heart and mind that somehow he had not been trusted enough to have been given a more visible leadership position. He worried that he didn't qualify for more trust. He saw the lack of position as lack of personal worthiness or ability.

I thought to myself, "This elder was one of the best—if I were asked to name the top group of missionaries in our mission experience, he would be near the top on that list."

I took the opportunity to review a list of his companions and assignments. That brought back memories and I remembered many soul-searching nights when I wondered how to help a specific homesick missionary or one who hadn't learned that the powers of heaven were connected to the level of his obedience. I thought of how much time and energy were devoted to the few missionaries with problems. I loved all of our missionaries and wanted them all to have a positive experience in their service to the Lord. Several times I was concerned that we might have to send a problem missionary home or that a discouraged missionary wouldn't bounce back and be effective.

I felt gratitude in remembering on two or three occasions the Lord had given an answer to my desire to bless those struggling by assigning this elder to serve as their companion. I even remembered that he was on my list to serve as my assistant on one occasion, yet the Lord had known that another elder needed his positive influence more than I needed him as an assistant.

I answered that wonderful, remarkable, and amazing missionary, "Elder, I'm pretty sure the Lord doesn't rank his children. But if I were asked to do so, considering our 563 missionaries of the Chile Santiago North Mission during our service, I would rank you in the top one or two percent. Do you remember your companions?" I queried. "One of them has maintained contact with me over the past years, and his mission and his life was changed because of his time with you. Elder, the Lord and I could trust you to 'do it the Lord's way'! You were exceptional."

No, I don't think the Lord ranks His children, but I do believe He knows who He can trust. If we don't get an answer to a heartfelt prayer, we should humbly thank Father for His trust in us and then move our feet, using our best judgment, to do what we feel He would want us to do. Perhaps no clear answer is the answer that He trusts us.

Prayer Self-Examination

1. Think of prayers you've been offering and the needs you've asked for help on. Have you wondered if your Father in Heaven is hearing you? Could it be that He trusts you to find your own answer? Have you submitted to Him how you intend to proceed?

2. What evidence is there in your life that Father in Heaven trusts you?

3. What do you think it will take to earn more trust from Heavenly Father?

Scriptures for Consideration and Marking

Proverbs 3:5	Helaman 10:4–5
Alma 26:11–13	2 Nephi 4:34

A Parting Thought

The scriptures are full of references that teach us to have trust in God and to refrain from putting our trust in the arm of flesh. It would be a pity for us—in some sort of self-serving manner—to think that since God can trust us, we can have an over-inflated trust in ourselves and thus diminish or discount our trust in Him. When we are trustworthy (worthy of being trusted), He can give us more stewardship over our lives. However, we are never excused from placing our trust in Him. Trust begets trust. I suggest we should always subscribe to Nephi's declaration when he said, "O Lord, I have trusted in thee, and I will trust in thee forever. I will not put my trust in the arm of flesh; for I know that cursed is he that putteth his trust in the arm of flesh. Yea, cursed is he that putteth his trust in man or maketh flesh his arm" (2 Nephi 4:34).

3

Only in Time of Crisis

"If prayer is only a spasmodic cry at the time of crisis, then it is utterly selfish, and we come to think of God as a repairman, or a service agency to help us only in our emergencies." (Howard W. Hunter, "Hallowed Be Thy Name," *Ensign*, November 1977, 52)

I remember reading a study in one of the leading newspapers in the United States on the subject of why people pray. The essence of the study was that people in trouble are more likely to pray than people who live status quo.

I recall public invitations, even by our prophets, to pray for rain so that crops could be saved. I even recall a national day of prayer for the concerns associated with the tragic events following the 9/11 terrorist activity, which resulted in the destruction of the World Trade Center in New York City.

As I look deeply at my own life or the lives of those I am closest to, it seems that prayer life can change quickly between intensity and casualness. When we are in need, we ask—even beg. When we are content with life, we become more complacent.

One beautiful fall evening in Gilbert, Arizona, my wife and I were attending a dinner at the home of one of the members of our ward. We left our five small children with a capable babysitter. Our oldest child, Chantel (who was eight years old at the time), is a special needs child who doesn't speak.

As we were beginning our dinner and engaging in friendly table conversation, the host informed me that one of my children was on the telephone. Our second child, six years old, said, "Daddy, we can't find Chantel anywhere and the babysitter asked me to call you while she is looking." While I was not overly concerned, I excused myself and went home. We looked for Chantel in every nook, corner, and closet of our home without success. It was dark outside, but I thought to check the yard. I was spiritually nudged to check the neighbors' yard first since they had a swimming pool. They were away. I found the first of three security gates to the yard and pool open. The second and third gates were also open. It was dark and the beautiful fall moon reflected its light off the still water of the pool. I couldn't see very well as I walked around the pool and could only detect what looked to be a skiff of dirt or sand on the bottom of the deep end. Relieved, I started to leave the pool area but then felt an impression to turn on the pool light to make one final inspection. With the help of the light, I could see that what I had thought to be dirt in the bottom of the pool was, in fact, Chantel's brown hair—she was lying still on the bottom!

I jumped frantically into the pool and retrieved her little body, believing it too late to do anything about this tragedy. Unknown to me, my wife had left the dinner and come home to help. She arrived in time to hear my anguished cries to heaven.

While my sweetheart administered CPR, I gave our firstborn a priesthood blessing. She began to breathe irregularly but remained unconscious. An ambulance was called, and many hours were spent in the critical care unit of the hospital, but finally, in a few days we were able to return home. She is alive and continues to bless us to this day, thirty-two years after the incident.

From the moment we thought she was lost, through the seventy-two-plus hours until we brought her home, our prayer life was intense. We were in distress. We were helpless and needed comfort. Our prayer life was impassioned. I know that was normal as it should have been. However, I ask myself about the intensity, frequency, and commitment of my prayers both before and after that crisis moment. Personal examination of my prayer life tells me I can do better.

How is it with you? Do you find in your own relationship with Heavenly Father that it's easy to drop off in your communications when the game of life seems pretty good? Do you find your prayer life vastly different when life's interruptions drive you to your knees? While that may be normal, perhaps we should consider the words and teachings of President Hunter at the start of this chapter.

Do we really want to develop the same relationship with our Heavenly Father as we do with our TV repairman or plumber? Can that kind of a relationship demonstrate an unhealthy dose of self-concern? Is the quantity and quality of our prayer life dictated by the magnitude of our needs or the intensity of our emergencies?

I have a testimony that, while my prayers don't need to have the same intensity as that moonlit night in Arizona, I do need a more careful relationship with my Heavenly Father than my specialty repairman or urgent care doctor. It is my witness that as we develop a close relationship with the Father of our spirits, He and His Son and the Holy Ghost will be as personal attending physicians, who watch over and bless us with tender mercies and divine signatures both in times of acute need and during our day-to-day living.

Prayer Self-Examination

1. When you consider your own prayers, do you find that they are dominated by those things that are in crisis mode in your life?

2. Approximately what percent of your prayer time is spent in requesting help for your own personal needs? Think about it. Would an audit of your prayers be more about your own needs and crisis or the needs and urgencies of others?

3. How could your prayer life improve by expanding your relationship with Heavenly Father beyond urgent requests and service calls?

Scriptures for Consideration and Marking

Psalm 75:1	Mosiah 24:22
Chronicles 16:8	Alma 8:22

A Parting Thought

As we seek to improve our prayer life, let's be sure to remember that the Lord asks us to request help—He wants us to ask. President Hunter did not counsel against seeking God's help in pressing times. He does suggest that if our prayers are all about our own urgent matters and do not include gratitude for the blessings we have or consider the needs of others, then they become selfish and self-centered. I have noticed that in the crisis moments of Lehi's family or when Ammon is captured by the Lamanites or when Old and New Testament apostles and prophets prayed in their times of crisis—they gave thanks. Gratitude discounts or deflects the tendency to be selfish. In the hours leading up to the Atonement and Crucifixion—His greatest personal extremity—Jesus "took the cup, and when he had given thanks, he gave it to them: and they all drank of it" (Mark 14:23). With this mind-set, God our Father becomes the giver, the protector, and carries our load because He loves us. We are less likely to consider Him as our butler or servant. He does not slide into the role of repairman or service agency. Instead He is our trusting, loving, and caring friend who desires the best for us and wants to bless us.

4

Allowing Our Weaknesses to Keep Us from Connecting with Heaven

"We may be too embarrassed to bring before the Lord specific weaknesses we have, yet he knows of them anyway. We thus prevent ourselves from gathering and gaining the strength we might need to overcome them. Admitting aloud (though in private) our weaknesses and stating our promises is sometimes better than just thinking them. Dealing with our specific weaknesses is far better than simply praying that we will be more righteous." (Neal A. Maxwell, "Prayer" [Salt Lake City: Deseret Book, 1977], 51)

I spent the first part of my younger life building walls. My dad was a masonry contractor. That's what we did every day—we built walls. With brick or cinder block and mortar, we built retaining walls, partitions, veneers, and fences. I was particularly moved when I read the following words written by Elder Burke Peterson when he wrote about the walls we sometimes build between ourselves and heaven—walls that prevent us from feeling we are being heard when we pray.

As we go through life, we oft times build a rock wall between ourselves and heaven. This wall is built by our unrepentant sins. For example, in our wall there may be stones of many different sizes and shapes. There could be stones because we have been unkind to someone. Criticism of leaders or teachers maybe add another stone. A lack of forgiveness may add another. Vulgar thoughts and actions may add some rather large stones in this wall. Dishonesty will add another; selfishness, another, and so on.

In spite of the wall we build in front of us, when we cry out to the Lord, he still sends his messages from heaven; but instead of being able to penetrate our hearts, they hit the wall that we have built up and bounce off. His messages don't penetrate, so we say "He doesn't hear," or "He doesn't answer." Sometimes this wall is very formidable, and the great challenge of life is to destroy it, or, if you please, to cleanse ourselves, purify the inner vessel so that we can be in tune with the Spirit. . . .

Those of you who may have some particular difficult experiences may only want to ask Him for the desire to pray. That may be all you want to ask for tonight. But at least ask that—a desire to pray. Then plead with Him, enjoy His Spirit, tell Him you love Him. I don't know how many of you have prayed out loud and in that vocal prayer have told the Lord you love Him, but that is a great experience.

After you have talked to Him, listen to Him. You must listen carefully, or you are going to miss His answers. Sometimes people pray for a minute or two, or five, or fifteen, and then not even listen for a second. Perhaps something different would happen if you continued to kneel at your chair or your bed (after you have prayed) for a minute or two, or five, or fifteen minutes until you get that good warm feeling that you have received an answer. Then you know the Lord has heard your prayer, you know He's there, and you know that you have finally found a way to allow Him to get His messages through to you. A great experience comes to those who feel the Spirit. (H. Burke Peterson, "Prayer—Try Again," *Ensign*, June 1981, 72–75)

Today would be a good day to do a "wall check." Maybe our walls will need to be taken down block by block over time. Perhaps we need to simply demolish the wall altogether with a wrecking ball. It's possible with strategy and heaven's help to remodel the wall with sufficient new window openings to allow the light to shine through and to encourage a new flow of divine air to come in. I have learned that it is one thing to concede that we have weaknesses and clearly another thing to lay them at the feet of our Savior and Redeemer and forsake them. Many times our weaknesses are an overextension of our strengths. Jehovah taught the Brother of Jared "And if men come unto me I will show unto them their weakness" (Ether 12:27). Our Lord and Savior will show us our weakness because He further instructs the Brother of Jared, "I give unto men weakness that they may be humble." Isn't that interesting? The Lord teaches that He gives us weakness for the specific purpose of helping us become aware that we need Him to help us change. Then we come to understand that His grace is able to remove the walls between us and heaven and turn those weaknesses into strengths. Admitting our specific weaknesses to the Lord (since He already knows them) and taking steps to overcome them will alter the walls sufficiently for us to create an effective connection to heaven.

Prayer Self–Examination

1. Are you willing to do a wall check? Are there any walls you have allowed to be erected in your life that have reduced the quality of your connection with Heavenly Father? If so, write them down.
2. What will it take to tear them down?
3. What can you do to keep the walls from being rebuilt?

Scriptures for Consideration and Marking

Helaman 17:7	3 Nephi 11:29
Alma 42:4	Ether 12:27

A Parting Thought

The walls that deflect answers from heaven, or keep us from feeling the peace that the Holy Ghost can give, are most often a result of our offending the Spirit. I have learned that the Spirit is easily offended. Contention, an unclean thought, a negative attitude, or even the slightest refusal to repent daily all facilitate the formation of a wall. Therefore, resisting contention with those around us will help to keep wall foundation stones from being formed. Finding ways to turn our attention from unholy thoughts will eliminate or remove blocks. We can find music or lyrics to hymns or Primary songs that chase away debilitating thoughts from the stage of our minds. Negative attitudes can arise from unthankful feelings. The network or cable news channels can become cesspools that breed negative attitudes about the government or economic conditions of the world. I love keeping up with current affairs, and I love to watch the news. However, I have learned that it is sometimes prudent to turn off the television or radio and reduce my diet of negativity. If we have resisted repenting daily, we must count the cost of continuing in our errors. We can scan our lives for chinks in our armor and foolish acts or words and then repent.

5

Raising Our Children on Our Knees

"Parents can offer a unique and wonderful kind of prayer because they are praying to the Eternal Parent of us all. There is great power in a prayer that essentially says, 'We are steward-parents over Thy children, Father; please help us to raise them as Thou wouldst want them raised.'" (M. Russell Ballard, "Daughters of God," *Ensign*, May 2008, 110)

I don't know whether you are a parent or not. But I do know that parents seldom, if ever, come to that responsibility with great experience and training. Most often we come to parenthood with a desire to raise up great children but feel unqualified to perform those duties. We soon learn that parenthood is more than changing diapers; making the rules; and watching our children safely move through infancy, toddlerhood, childhood, and teenage years. We find that parenting is a twenty-four-hour, seven-days-a-week concern. Parents learn that all family home evenings are not as spiritual as portrayed on Church video programs. While family scripture study can be inspiring, the truth is that at times we would really like to uninvite one or more of the children to participate, because of disruptive distractions. Our love and reason can be sapped by tiredness and worry when a teenage daughter stays out late and violates the family rule of being in by midnight. Bottom line, being a parent is not for the faint hearted and not only for those who have lots of training in child development and family relations. Parenthood is a challenging commandment—for Father commands that each married couple "multiply and replenish the earth" (Genesis 1:28).

The loving Parent of us all does not leave us alone in the most important role we will ever play in this life. He invites us to keep Him involved in the joint stewardship of blessing His children who are on loan to us.

My dad and mom were extraordinary parents. I think most who know them well would agree. However, they would also count them as pretty ordinary people. Dad was a farmer turned masonry contractor. While he was faithful and appropriately devout in his religion, he served on a high council but never as a bishop or any other visible callings until being called as a patriarch in his final years. His time on the dairy farm—with cows switching their tails across his brow or knocking off his hat—likely influenced his vocabulary with a few simple swear words, which he later had to reform. Mom was a wonderful little lady, who had tremendous faith. She was an outstanding cook and gardener and had the capacity to show her love through her homemade bread and treats or with beautiful flowers.

On several occasions I've heard people say, "Vaughn and Irene, you've got nine children, and they've all done well in the things that matter most. How did you do it?" Their answer was always very simple: "We were just a couple of kids and didn't know anything. I guess you could say that we just raised our kids on our knees."

Elder Ballard's words invite us as parents to "raise our children on our knees." Praying for our children is important, but praying for their parents is also important. We must ask our Eternal Father to bless us, to temper our hearts, to help us avoid unhealthy pride, to give us discernment, and simply to help us know how to respond to them and our challenges in raising them. Praying for them and praying that our actions as parents—even those that in retrospect could have been better—will be consecrated for the good of our children.

Prayer Self-Examination

1. If you have children or a spouse, are you praying for them daily? If you don't have children yet, are you praying for their parents? If you aren't married yet, do you pray for your spouse? Someday future loved ones will call you sweetheart, mom, or dad. Now is not too early to pray for them.

2. Do your prayers about children often include a phrase like "Father, this is your child and you know what's

best for her. As a steward over her, help me to treat her in the way thou wouldst have me do"?

3. Do you ask Heavenly Father to consecrate or make holy your actions as a parent to the well-being of the child? And do you ask that the results (positive or negative) will be consecrated for your good as a parent—to help you learn how to do better next time?

4. Do you thank Father in Heaven for the opportunity to share in this part of His family plan?

Scriptures for Consideration and Marking

Moroni 8:3   D&C 68:25
Moroni 7:48

A Parting Thought

Being a parent has to be one of the most challenging and most wonderful experiences we have while on this earth. Someone once said that the greatest joys as well as the greatest sorrows of life are in family relationships. I've found that to be true. Without question, the greatest joys I've experienced are in seeing and feeling the blessing of worthy children and righteous parents and siblings. The greatest sorrows are also in these same relationships—when a child or loved one resists or rejects receiving the blessings that God promises to His worthy children. I have a testimony that God loves His children—all of them. When we acknowledge Him and His love in every facet of the family relationship, He blesses us with insight and understanding, which helps us to successfully have joy and to learn from our challenges. I love the scripture where Mormon describes his feelings in a written letter for his son Moroni saying, "I am mindful of you always in my prayers, continually praying unto God the Father in the name of his Holy Child, Jesus, that he, through his infinite goodness and grace, will keep you through the endurance of faith on his name to the end" (Moroni 8:3). May our prayers always demonstrate that we are mindful of our children, their parents, and the Father's role in each of our lives.

6

Not a Stranger but a Friend

"The minute a man stops supplicating God for his spirit and direction, just so soon he starts to become a stranger to him and his works. When men stop praying for God's Spirit, they place confidence in their own unaided reason, and they gradually lose the spirit of God, just the same as near and dear friends, by never writing to or visiting with each other, will become strangers." (Heber J. Grant, *Improvement Era*, August 1944)

I have been favored in my life with good friends. I hope you have too. Ralph Waldo Emerson wrote, "We take care of our health, we lay up our money; we make tight our roof and our clothing sufficient, but who provides wisely that he shall not be wanting in the best property of all—friends." It's true, isn't it? I have known some of my friends for nearly fifty years. Though we may not see each other often, we exchange emails and phone calls. When we are blessed to be in one another's presence, it's like we were never apart. We pick up on conversation and reminisce of days gone by like they were yesterday. During our visits and communication, we remember birthdays and talk of our lives and circumstances. Love, common interests, and mutual admiration nurtured with periodic contact is sufficient to provide us with true friendship.

I contrast those relationships with many other good people I've crossed paths with over the years. In the seasons of our friendship I felt equally close to them in our common daily pursuit. While I have positive memories of them, the effect of no contact, no association, and no dealings have rendered a distant relationship. If we were to cross paths again, we may not even recognize each other.

President Heber J. Grant teaches that our connection with Father in Heaven will likewise be disconnected if we will begin to rely on other pseudo means to find answers. Reasoning of the mind will take over, and spiritual estrangement will put us on our own.

What a tragic way to go. Separated, divorced, estranged from Father in Heaven. Though He will never lose His love and care for us, if we distance ourselves from Him through separation and antipathy, it is as though we don't know Him at all. We lose the blessing, benefit, and joy that comes from being close friends with Him.

I have a testimony that prayer allows us to stay close to Him. It is interesting to note the first doctrinal concept taught to those investigating the Church (see *Preach My Gospel*, 31): "We have a Heavenly Father who loves us." Early in the missionary effort to bring the restored gospel to others is to insure that those being taught are praying. If not, then we seek to reconnect them with

Heavenly Father through prayer. The Bible Dictionary states, "As soon as we learn the true relationship in which we stand toward God (namely, God is our Father, and we are his children), then at once prayer becomes natural and instinctive on our part. Many of the so-called difficulties about prayer arise from forgetting this relationship. Prayer is the act by which the will of the Father and the will of the child are brought into correspondence with each other."

Developing and maintaining a relationship with anyone requires attention and effort. There is a certain amount of work entailed in writing emails, making phone calls, and finding time to visit friends. Maintaining our connection and renewing our desire to remain true friends is the only way we will maintain our relationship. Likewise, daily prayer and remembering the nature of our Father in Heaven and His love for us is a must in maintaining and benefitting from our connection to Him.

Prayer Self-Examination

1. Can you feel Heavenly Father's love for you? Do you know that He is your Father and that you are His child? Do you know and feel that He wants to bless you and help you progress? He knows you—do you feel like you know Him?

2. Meditation, pondering, and remembering Him are forms of informal prayer. How do you keep your connection strong with Him?

3. What will you do to strengthen your relationship with Him?

Scriptures for Consideration and Marking

1 Nephi 18:3	Proverbs 15:29
Enos 1:4	Matthew 7:7–11

A Parting Thought

I have found when I can think of Heavenly Father in the same way that I think of my earthly father (or a mentor I trust and love), then I feel a closeness with Him. Like my own father, I have come to feel that my Father in Heaven knows me. He wants me to grow up to be like Him. He listens when I talk and seldom preaches to me. My earthly father always tried to make me feel like I was somebody special. He gave me experiences that prepared me to take responsibility on the family farm or to take a role in his construction business. My Heavenly Father knows that I can become like Him. He too gives me experiences and training so that I can take on more of His attributes. He is no stranger to me. I love Him and I know that He loves me.

7

Pray Always!

"Morning and evening prayers—and all of the prayers in between—are not unrelated, discrete events; rather, they are linked together each day and across days, weeks, months, and even years. This is in part how we fulfill the scriptural admonition to 'pray always.' Such meaningful prayers are instrumental in obtaining the highest blessings God holds in store for His faithful children." (David A. Bednar, "Pray Always," *Ensign*, Nov. 2008)

I like to think of my morning and evening prayers as the bookends of my day. In the morning I thank Him for my restful night sleep (or tell Him about it if I didn't have such a great sleep). Throughout the day, I consult with Him (mostly on an informal basis) regarding the happenings of the day. I try to be sure to say "I thank thee" as many times as I recognize His hand in my doings. When things become perplexing and don't turn out as I had hoped, then I invite Him to help me see things more clearly so that I can make adjustments. I always like to invite insight and ask Him to bless me with sudden strokes of inspiration, nudges toward the correct path, and stirring of my soul and mind to keep it fresh and lucid.

Another way to look at it is that at least twice daily we have a formal interview with our Father and an opportunity to seek advice, initiate action, and report on our execution. In our day, the process of digital communication allows us to stay connected with others. Through texting, we can give short thoughts and ideas as well as report progress in short word bites. Similarly throughout our day, we can "text" our Heavenly Father through short expressions of gratitude, invitations for new insight, and to let Him know when we've completed step-by-step actions leading us toward some desired goal. A friend of mine recently shared with me, "I used to remember something during the day that I forgot to include in my morning prayers and committed to remember it for my nightly prayers. This counsel gave me permission to continue my prayers right then and there." As we pray formally twice or more times daily and continue throughout the day with informal expressions of gratitude and supplication for help, we stay connected and fulfill divine counsel to pray always or pray oft.

I am instructed by the words of Amulek when he taught,

> Therefore may God grant unto you, my brethren, that ye may begin to exercise your faith unto repentance, that ye begin to call upon his holy name, that he would have mercy upon you;

Yea, cry unto him for mercy; for he is mighty to save.

Yea, humble yourselves, and continue in prayer unto him.

Cry unto him when ye are in your fields, yea, over all your flocks.

Cry unto him in your houses, yea, over all your household, both morning, mid-day, and evening.

Yea, cry unto him against the power of your enemies.

Yea, cry unto him against the devil, who is an enemy to all righteousness.

Cry unto him over the crops of your fields, that ye may prosper in them.

Cry over the flocks of your fields, that they may increase.

But this is not all; ye must pour out your souls in your closets, and your secret places, and in your wilderness.

Yea, and when you do not cry unto the Lord, let your hearts be full, drawn out in prayer unto him continually for your welfare, and also for the welfare of those who are around you. (Alma 34:17–27)

Our prayers can be a continual conversation with Heavenly Father throughout the day. He's invited us to talk to Him about anything and everything. As we talk to Him about our work, school, relationships, challenges, successes, wonderings, and everything, we more completely follow His admonition to "counsel with the Lord in all thy doings" and to "let all thy doings be unto the Lord, and whithersoever thou goest let it be in the Lord; yea, let all thy thoughts be directed unto the Lord" (Alma 37:35–37). Then Alma tells Helaman the benefit that comes from that kind of prayer life when he says "and he will direct thee for good."

Prayer Self-Examination

1. Have you developed good "bookend" prayer habits? Morning and evening prayers?
2. Do you find yourself in short informal prayer often throughout the day?
3. When you text another person you generally anticipate a response. In your informal prayer life, are you getting those short answers (revelations) from the Lord to help shape your day? If not, what would it take to improve that kind of communication?

Scriptures for Consideration and Marking

2 Nephi 32:9	D&C 10:5
3 Nephi 18:19	D&C 19:38
Ephesians 6:18	D&C 90:24

A Parting Thought

The quality of our prayer life is measured by the value we place on our morning and evening prayer complemented by frequent short informal prayers. Too frequently today in the work place, entertainment, and simple everyday conversation, we hear the names God and Christ taken in vain and used in course and lewd ways. This is not prayer and should be forever offensive. However, in quiet respectful and reverent ways (mostly in the mind and heart) we can frequently call our Father. The Lord wants us to remember Him in all things. He counsels "that your incomings may be in the name of the Lord; that your outgoings may be in the name of the Lord; that all your salutations may be in the name of the Lord" (D&C 88:120, 109:9). Praying always requires that we call on Him in the name of the Son and acknowledge Him in all things.

8

Keep Them Simple

"Do our prayers at times sound and feel the same? Have you ever said a prayer mechanically, the words pouring forth as though cut from a machine? Do you sometimes bore yourself as you pray? Will prayers that do not demand much of your thought merit much attention from our Heavenly Father? When you find yourself getting into a routine with your prayers, step back and think. Meditate for a while on the things for which you really are grateful. Look for them. They don't have to be grand or glorious. Sometimes we should express our gratitude for the small and simple things like the scent of rain, the taste of your favorite food, or the sound of a loved one's voice." (Joseph B. Wirthlin, Devotional Address, Brigham Young University, January 21, 2003)

I enjoy doing word studies. Often I like to look at the words in a scripture and take a deeper look into what those words mean. Many times I find new understanding by seeing how those words combine. Let's examine Elder Wirthlin's word use and consider his quote in search for an expanded meaning. A few of the words include:

Mechanical: robotic, automated, unthinking, unconscious, involuntary, without emotion, unfeeling, lifeless, perfunctory, cursory, careless, casual

Bore: tire, fatigue, send to sleep, leave cold, bore to death, bore to tears, informal turn off, dull, bother, yawn

Routine: procedure, practice, pattern, drill, regimen, program, schedule, plan, formula, method, system, customs, habitual

Meditate: contemplate, think, consider, ponder, muse, reflect, deliberate, ruminate, brood, mull something over, be deep/lost in thought, debate with oneself, pray, informally put on one's thinking cap, informally cogitate

Look: examination, study, inspection, observation, scan, survey, peep, peek, glimpse, gaze, stare, an informal eyeful, gander, look-see

Simple: unpretentious, unsophisticated, ordinary, unaffected, unassuming, natural, uncomplicated, accessible, without much decoration

One of the primary purposes of personal daily prayer is to meaningfully connect us with heaven. Now carefully reread Elder Wirthlin's quote at the start of this section. He encourages us to consider our prayers in light of whether they are robotic and without feeling. Cursory and casual prayers, offered without consciousness, are not really prayers at all. If during our prayers, we tire, are inclined to sleep, or dull our own senses, we need to stop and think. The routine of prayer in our bookend (morning and evening) prayers can also invite habitual language and a system of praying for the same things in the same way day-after-day. We can easily fall into a mindless checklist of following a procedure of programmed wording. Sometimes our prayers can be recited in a pattern without thought or reflection.

Elder Wirthlin invites us to contemplate, think, and ponder. We should examine, study, and inspect what we pray about. As we do we may find that the most important things to be thankful for are those that may seem insignificant and even inconsequential. We may find our most precious gifts are those that are most ordinary and uncomplicated as well as accessible—if we pay attention.

I love Elder Wirthlin. I have appreciated his wisdom and unassuming way. Simplicity is his signature and unpretentious is his nature. His counsel on prayer reflects the same.

Prayer Self-Examination

1. Do your prayers feel and sound the same? Are the phrases you use, either in private or public, predictable?
2. Do you think about what you are saying? Can you find different ways of saying what you feel?
3. When you do catch yourself in vain repetitions, do you stop and consider what you are praying for?
4. Next time you pray, see if you can identify three to five small and simple things that have blessed your life during the day, and express gratitude for them.

Scriptures for Consideration and Marking

3 Nephi 13:7	3 Nephi 19:24
Matthew 6:7	Alma 33:7
1 Corinthians 14:15	3 Nephi 19:34

A Parting Thought

We began this chapter with the words and counsel of Elder Wirthlin. I use his words to conclude this chapter as well. He said,

> The rich blessings that can come into our lives through prayer are available to all. The poor have as much access as the rich. The movie star has no more advantage over the laborer. We are all equal in our ability to approach the throne of our Heavenly King. . . . As we approach our Heavenly Father in the name of Christ, we open the windows of heaven. . . . Prayer is the doorway through which we commence our discipleship to things heavenly and eternal. We will never be alone so long as we know how to pray. (Joseph B. Wirthlin, Devotional Address Brigham Young University, January 21, 2003)

As we learn how to keep our prayer life a connecting force in our relationship with God our Father, may we develop a greater capacity to communicate in fresh and thoughtful language and express gratitude for the tender mercies and divine signatures He gives to us.

9

Behold an Open Door

"Prayer begins with individual initiative. 'Behold,' saith the Lord, 'I stand at the door, and knock: if any man hear my voice, and open the door, I will come in to him, and will sup with him, and he with me.' That door is opened when we pray to our Heavenly Father in the name of Jesus Christ." (Russell M. Nelson, "Lessons from the Lord's Prayers," *Ensign*, May 2009)

When someone knocks on the outside of a door, it is a request to be acknowledged and invited to enter. When a person picks up a telephone, and calls a specific number and hears a ring tone, he initiates a definite summons for the receiver to answer and open communication. All of us understand and perform these practices on a daily basis.

I have noticed that with caller identification systems, which are common today, the recipient of the call can immediately identify the caller. The recipient chooses whether or not to pick up and answer. The practice can be frustrating to others, yet we all use it to manage the busyness of life. We use agency to choose. Every missionary, home teacher, and visiting teacher can verify that some people refuse to answer a ringing door bell or a distinct knock on the door. Think of the blessing these servants of God carry with them—a message of joy, happiness, and eternal peace—something that can change a life forever. Yet the person on the other side of the door chooses not to open his door or heart. Heartbreaking, isn't it?

When the Lord says "behold," He is saying "Look! I have something for you" or "see what I have" or "observe what you can receive" (or view, watch, survey, witness, gaze upon, regard, contemplate, or inspect what I can do for you). After the Lord invites us to consider His presence and love, He states in simple terms "I'm knocking on the door" or "I'm calling you." All we need to do to activate the blessing of being connected to Him is to pick up the phone or answer the door. It doesn't get any more difficult than that. We must respond to the knock or the ring. Elder Nelson reminds us that Heavenly Father is already there and invites us to respond to His love and care by communicating through praying.

Sometimes it is easy to think of it in the opposite way. We might have the incorrect notion that it is we who knock on His door or rings His telephone. We could even erroneously think that it is He who chooses not to answer our call or open the door. We may try to put the blame on Him if we feel disconnected. That is simply untrue. The Father and the Son stand at the door and have already knocked. They've already programmed in our number and the invitation for us to respond has already been delivered. It is we who must "do" in order to connect with the Father through and in the name of His Son Jesus Christ.

Sometimes, we may think we open the door or answer His call by our cursory prayers or feeble attempts to connect with Him. The Bible Dictionary states, "Prayer is a form of work and is an appointed means for obtaining the highest of all blessings." Receiving His calls or responding to the knock on our door is not a passive action; it is work. It is a labor that requires effort, maybe a little sweat, and sustained exertion. If we go about it lazily, it's possible that our connection to heaven will not come. We must always remember that the benefits of a powerful connection to Heavenly Father far outweigh the lazy way and allow us to feast with Him. It is worth whatever effort we must expend to connect with Him through prayer by opening the door on our end.

Prayer Self-Examination

1. What does working at our prayers look like?
2. Can you think of times when you felt your response to the Lord's invitation to open the door or answer His call opened a connection with Heaven? What did you do to merit the connection? If you've never had such an experience, what do you think it would take to demonstrate your desire to connect with the powers of heaven?
3. Are you willing to imagine the Father and His Son being just outside the door or waiting for you to answer a call with a desire to connect? Will you do it?

Scriptures for Consideration and Marking

Revelation 3:20	D&C 49:26
D&C 14:5	3 Nephi 14:7
D&C 4:7	Luke 11:9

A Parting Thought

This principle can revolutionize our prayer life. Contrast it with the common thought that prayer is an act where we kneel down in attitude of reverence and in essence, knock on the door of the Lord to thank Him and seek guidance, then close the door. When Joseph Smith read the scripture in James 1:5, it was the Lord knocking on Joseph's door. The knock motivated Joseph to go into the grove to open the door through prayer. His simple prayer was an action—even a labor—to respond to the knock. Joseph did not knock on the door of God to get an answer, but rather he responded to the Lord's knock and answered by offering up a heartfelt prayer. Joseph's prayer rendered an answer that included the Father, the Son, and without doubt the Holy Ghost. Think of the power of it—when you visualize God the Father and His Son Jesus Christ and the Holy Ghost standing at the door inviting you to answer. Instead of beggars going to His door for sustenance, we open the door to a loving trinity of Gods who have invited us to partake of their nourishment and support. The dynamics of our relationship changes.

To be clear, God is our Father, Jesus Christ is our Savior and King, and the Holy Ghost is our Comforter and Teacher. The Holy Ghost is the means provided to guide, direct, and speak answers to our prayers. I am grateful to know that They invite the connection by knocking on my door. I have a testimony that They stand ready to answer if we will but open the door or receive the call.

10

Timing: A Divine Perspective

"The answers to our prayers come in the Lord's due time. Sometimes we may become frustrated that the Lord has delayed answering our prayers. In such times we need to understand that He knows what we do not know. He sees what we do not see. Trust in Him. He knows what is best for His child, and being a perfect God, He will answer our prayers perfectly and in the perfect time." (Dieter F. Uchtdorf, "Prayer and the Blue Horizon," *Ensign*, June 2009, 6)

Someone once said hindsight is 20/20. In other words, it is often easier to judge a situation when we have all the information and can see the whole picture. Most of us can look back on times or conditions when we felt used, abused, paralyzed, frustrated, or fully perplexed about life. However, at a later time, we can see that the Lord had His hand in our lives all along. We can see that—with His all-knowing eye, combined with His mission and purpose to bring to pass the greatest good—He allows everything to work out perfectly in the end.

At the start of our marriage, my wife and I uttered many prayers that were centered around our future family. We petitioned the Lord for the blessing of valiant children who would love Him. We prayed that we would be prepared to teach them and that they would be blessed with experiences to edify and increase their capacity to be compassionate and loving builders of His kingdom. We told Him we would be happy to receive as many children as He felt to entrust with us. The months passed, and we were blessed with a baby girl. She was pink, beautiful, and perfect. We named her Chantel. We loved observing her growth and progress. Those were special moments when she grabbed her daddy's big nose and said "Da-Da" or responded to my wife with a bright smile and cuddled into the nape of her neck to reciprocate love. We taught her to recognize the pictures of Jesus; "Jee-Sus" she would say, pointing to artwork prints on the walls of our home and at church. Around eighteen months of age, we noticed that she wasn't saying "Da-Da" or "Mommy" or "Jesus" anymore. In fact, she wasn't saying anything. She often had what appeared to be painful crying spells; she did not try to communicate. We detected that something was not right and sought to find an answer to this delay of progress. We commenced down a road that lasted for years with many doctors and multitudes of prayers and priesthood blessings, often having our hopes dashed and expectations shattered along the way.

A few years passed, and Creshel and Aaron joined our little family circle. These were interesting times with more diapers and all the work that comes with little ones, especially with Chantel's condition. I remember one night in particular when Chantel was about four years old. Well after midnight she began crying and my wife was unable to comfort or calm her. Around two o'clock I offered to take a turn. She liked to ride in the car, so I determined I would take her out for ride to see if that would soothe her. I took her to another room to change her wet diaper as she continued to scream. While doing so, I confess something I'm not proud of—I looked up and with outstretched arms and hands toward heaven, I distressfully demanded in a scolding tone, "What's going on?" In an attitude of frustration and even complaint, I questioned the Lord. Why were we not finding an answer. Little did we know the road ahead was long. We were just beginning, yet fatigue was already setting in.

I heard no audible voice, but a distinct memory flashed into my mind. I saw an image of a newlywed couple kneeling by their bedside praying for a valiant family, even a houseful of children who would be given experiences to bless them with compassion, testimonies, and a love for building Father's kingdom. An impression came into my mind and then transformed into words:"I am answering your prayers. You asked for a valiant family and I have given you a celestial child, as your first, to help you teach the others." At first I thought, "But this is not the blessing I had in mind." However I felt the magnitude of that teaching moment where Father was helping me to see something really important. I was ashamed and humbled. I asked for forgiveness for my frustrated, misbehaving attitude and questioning words. I committed to be more trusting and grateful.

Our professional pathway—which included many doctors and many methods promising a cure and many wonderful people helping—ultimately led us to Detroit, Michigan. At last, a doctor confirmed the diagnosis of Rett Syndrome (a progressive brain dysfunction. Ten years later in 1999, it was found to have a chromosomal cause). Now we had an understanding and a network to work within. By then Chalonn, Chelise, Chenae, Candra, and Devin had joined our family circle.

As I look from my 20/20 hindsight view, I can see that the prayers of that young couple were marvelously answered by the Lord. His timing in each element of my career path was impeccably leading us to answers to our medical dilemma. I have discovered that all our lives and experiences are intertwined for our good. Chantel has been a wonderful teacher to her parents and seven younger siblings. We have our faults of course, but I see how much of the good character and testimony of our seven other children can be traced to our teacher. I have a testimony that the Lord answered our newlywed prayers. Our family has been blessed with valiant children who are compassionate builders of the Lord's kingdom. I testify that we can trust the Lord in His timing and in His method.

A note: At this writing, Chantel still does not speak or have any self-help skills. She still requires constant care. And she continues to teach us all and has expanded her influence to friends, ward members, and community. She accompanied us to Chile when I presided over the Chile Santiago North Mission and extended her influence to 563 missionaries. She resided with our son Aaron and his family while I presided over the Guatemala MTC and had positive up close and personal impact upon her nephews and nieces.

Prayer Self–Examination

1. Have you had experiences where hindsight strengthens your testimony of the Lord's timing and method? If so, I invite you to share it with someone today—they may need your witness. Pick up the phone, write a note—share your testimony.

2. How can your prayers be modified and strengthened by remembering that the Lord has perfect timing and understands how to teach us and help us to grow?

3. Outside of your own personal experience, who do you know (personally or through the scriptures) who has learned that the Lord is mindful of us and gives us experiences for our good and our training? Consider writing about them in your journal.

Scriptures for Consideration and Marking

Isaiah 55:8–9   Abraham 3:19
1 Samuel 16:7   Proverbs 14:12
Jacob 4:8

A Parting Thought

I highlighted just one of many evidences in my own life that Heavenly Father's timing and method witness of His perfect love and desire for our well-being. My own witness includes getting typhoid fever while serving a mission in Mexico (very frustrating to me), which directly led to who and when I married. It includes cancelling plans the day before groundbreaking to build a new home in what seemed a perfect location and environment, which lead to an interview and subsequent call to serve as a mission president in a foreign land. I have literally scores of evidences seen through the window of hindsight that attest to the Lord's involvement in the details of my life. Knowing and remembering the Lord's involvement from the past experiences of our lives will help us successfully encounter, with faith, our challenges in the future.

11

God and Angels

"Whenever these moments of our extremity come, we must not succumb to the fear that God has abandoned us or that He does not hear our prayers. He does hear us. He does see us. He does love us. When we are in dire circumstances and want to cry, 'Where art Thou?' it is imperative that we remember He is right there with us—where He has always been! We must continue to believe, continue to have faith, continue to pray and plead with heaven, even if we feel for a time our prayers are not heard and that God has somehow gone away. He is there. Our prayers are heard. And when we weep He and the angels of heaven weep with us." (Jeffrey R. Holland, CES fireside given on September 7, 2008, Brigham Young University)

I recall a time when I was somewhere between being a little boy attached to Mother's apron strings and growing toward being a teen. I was learning that bigger boys became Boy Scouts who were—by their own law—trustworthy, loyal, helpful, friendly, courteous, kind, obedient, cheerful, thrifty, brave, clean, and reverent. I was consciously trying to be that kind of boy. However, one trait caused me some trouble, especially when we were on camping trips in the cougar country of northwestern New Mexico—being brave. I had a wonderful Scoutmaster who seemed to feel that scared and even terrified boys rather than boys who were fearless were easier to control at night.

One night around a campfire, this good Scoutmaster told us a story about an acquaintance who supposedly had encountered a cougar in the very area where we were camping. I will spare the details but, suffice it to say, his telling the story included not only the scream and sounds of cougars, but also the details of a bloody scuffle, a miraculous escape, and a trip to the hospital to get more than a hundred stitches. When he finished, he said, "Okay, boys, it's lights out—time to go to bed." We filed obediently to our tents. I positioned myself in the middle of two other Scouts in our three-man tent. The boy on my left went to the bottom of his sleeping bag and took the fetal position. The boy on my right lay stiff as a board asking me every few minutes if I'd heard the sound in the distant sand cliffs. That night was long. I was frightened but just "big boy" enough not to admit it, especially to my friends. Some moments during the night, I could hear my heart beating in my chest, and I wondered if I would ever be brave.

The boys in the other tent weren't so "big boy"; every half hour or so, one in particular would call out loudly to our Scoutmaster sleeping in his own tent, "Brother Sherman, is it time to get up yet?" Brother Sherman would patiently answer with enough words to console us. Somehow just knowing he was there was enough to inject a little more bravery into my new Scout heart. His being aware of us was adequate to prop up our bravery and fortify our courage. Though at times it seemed the night would never end, I managed to doze off several times and get a little sleep and respite from my vivid imagination. Finally the light in the east began to signal morning was arriving. Just a little light was enough to chase away the imagined cougars and give confidence that we could make it through the night unscathed. Over fifty years later and dozens of campouts later, I'm here to evidence that cougars, bears, snakes, spiders, or other imagined monsters never harmed us.

Through the challenges of earth life, our bravery is enhanced when we know that Father is there and that others are nearby who can bolster our courage and reinforce us.

I add my testimony to that of Elder Holland. God is near. Angels both seen and unseen, mortal and immortal, sustain and support us. I have seen the Lord's hand in many lives and know that we are not only aided by the Holy Ghost, but also by a Holy Host.

I have always loved the story of Elisha. A servant awoke early one morning to see the enemy with numerous soldiers and chariots surrounding them. It appeared they would be easily destroyed, and the servant inquired fearfully of Elisha, "What are we to do?"

Elisha answered, "Fear not: for they that be with us are more than they that be with them. And Elisha prayed, and said, Lord, I pray thee, open his eyes, that he may see. And the Lord opened the eyes of the young man; and he saw: and, behold, the mountain was full of horses and chariots of fire round about Elisha" (2 Kings 6:16–17).

Father is there. He hears and answers our prayers. We are assisted by angels. Pray to our Father and know He is there until the light can chase away our fears. Let the mortal angels, as well as those unseen, buoy us up and strengthen us.

Prayer Self-Examination

1. Are your prayers filled with faith that Father is there and is assisted by angels who can aid us with courage to carry on?

2. Who are the mortal angels who sustain you? Have you not only thanked Heavenly Father for them, but also expressed your appreciation to them personally?

3. Is there someone you know who needs assistance? Have you prayed to know how you might be able to be an answer to their prayers?

Scriptures for Consideration and Marking

| 2 Kings 6:16–17 | Mosiah 27:14 |
| Mosiah 9:18 | Moroni 7:29–31 |

A Parting Thought

In earlier chapters we discussed the blessing of knowing that our Father and Jesus Christ have knocked and are at the door waiting for us to take action and open the door. I have a strong testimony that we are never abandoned by the Father of our spirits. He loves us. He desires that the first principle of His gospel, faith, becomes the foundation of our relationship with Him. He wants our allegiance, loyalty, and trust. Wherever we are in our testimony of these foundational truths, I pray we will know that He is there and is answering our prayers. I know He allows others to execute His will to bless us with answers. May we be alert and perceptive in recognizing His answers, His agents, and opportunities to be an instrument in His hands.

12

Teach Them Early

"It is so important that parents call their children together night and morning, every day, and give each member of the family, one by one, the privilege of addressing the Lord on behalf of the family, expressing gratitude for the many blessings the family has received, and the concern for individual and family problems. It is important for each person to ask for guidance in the morning, with the knowledge that he will report at night. Children should learn early in life that they can call upon their Father in heaven." (N. Eldon Tanner, "Importance and Efficacy of Prayer," *Ensign*, Aug. 1971)

I am struck by the constant and consistent counsel of living prophets for families to gather in family prayer. Although President Tanner's message will be our lead quote for this chapter, let's review some of the teachings of other latter-day prophets.

President Heber J. Grant counseled,

> I am convinced that one of the greatest things that can come into any home to cause the boys and girls in that home to grow up in a love of God, and in a love of the

gospel of Jesus Christ, is to have family prayer. . . . I believe that there are very few that go astray, that very few lose their faith, who have once had a knowledge of the gospel, and who never neglect their prayers in their families, and their secret supplications to God. (Conference Report, Oct. 1923, 7–8)

President Kimball taught,

No mother would carelessly send her little children forth to school on a wintry morning without warm clothes to protect against the snow and rain and cold. But there are numerous fathers and mothers who send their children to school without the protective covering available to them through prayer—a protection against exposure to unknown hazards, evil people, and base temptations. (*Teachings of Spencer W. Kimball*, 122–23)

President Kimball continued with this caution:

When we kneel in family prayer, our children at our side on their knees are learning habits that will stay with them all through their lives. If we do not take time for prayers, what we are actually saying to our children is, "Well, it isn't very important, anyway. We won't worry about it. If we can do it conveniently, we will have our prayer, but if the school bell rings and the bus is coming and employment is calling—well, prayer isn't very important and we will do it when it is convenient." Unless planned for, it never seems to be convenient. (*Teachings of Spencer W. Kimball*, 117–18)

Elder Joe J. Christensen, then of the Presidency of the Seventy, taught this encouraging insight to parents: "Remember family prayer every day. With schedules as they are, you may need to have more than one prayer" ("Rearing Children in a Polluted Environment," *Ensign*, Nov. 1993, 12).

President Hinckley witnessed, "I give you my testimony that if you sincerely apply family prayer, you will not go away unrewarded. The changes may not be readily apparent. They may be extremely subtle. But they will be real, for God 'is a rewarder of them that diligently seek him'" ("The Blessings of Family Prayer," *Ensign*, Feb. 1991, 5).

President James E. Faust (using the example of a time when President Kimball interviewed a bishop) gave this admonition: "In the past, having family prayer once a day may have been all right. But in the future it will not be enough if we are going to save our families" ("The Greatest Challenge in the World—Good Parenting," *Ensign*, Nov. 1990, 33).

We are living in perilous times, which President Ezra Taft Benson cautioned members of the Church to remember: "Just a few words added to the blessing on the food, as is becoming the custom in some parts, is not enough. We need to get onto our knees in prayer and gratitude" (*The Teachings of Ezra Taft Benson* [Bookcraft, 1988], 460).

I love this counsel and promise from President Hinckley, which merits our attention. He said,

I know of no single practice that will have a more salutary effect upon your lives than the practice of kneeling together as you begin and close each day. Somehow the little storms that seem to afflict every marriage are dissipated when, kneeling before the Lord, you thank him for one another, in the presence of one another, and then together invoke his blessings upon your lives, your home, your loved ones, and your dreams. ("Except the Lord Build the House," *Ensign*, June 1971, 72)

The prophets have spoken. Counsel and advice has been delivered. We have been admonished and invited to either continue in our strong patterns of family prayer or to re-establish the practice as a cornerstone of our fight against the adversary. Could it be that one of the most basic remedies to check and control the erosion of personal character and the destruction of families is in consistent and meaningful family prayer? In the words of President Hinckley, "I feel satisfied that there is no adequate substitute for the morning and evening practice of kneeling together—father, mother, and children. This, more than soft carpets, more than lovely draperies, more than cleverly balanced color schemes, is the thing that will make for better and more beautiful homes" ("The Blessings of Family Prayer," *Ensign*, February 1991). Let us consider and examine our commitment to family prayer and make an effort to improve today.

Prayer Self-Examination

1. What is your current practice of family prayer? If you are able, do you kneel? When and how often do you pray as a family? Does each member of the family have an opportunity to act as voice?

2. What are the positive aspects of your family prayer life? What new or additional things can you add or discontinue to make your family prayer time better?

3. As you begin any new effort to improve, there will be opposition. Our efforts may not be rewarded as quickly as you hope. Are you willing to take this initiative on and persevere over the long haul? Will you keep trying?

Scriptures for Consideration and Marking

3 Nephi 18:21	2 Thessalonians 2:15
D&C 23:6	2 Timothy 3:1–4

A Parting Thought

My own parents blessed my life by teaching principles and practices. They are certainly among my greatest heroes and have impacted me in many important ways. When they died, they left a little economic inheritance, which was divided equally among their nine children. Those funds have been spent or invested, but in the end they will go the way of the rest our earthly possessions. We also received several little tokens and memoirs that remind us of their faithfulness to the Lord, keeping covenants and being disciples. However, I know of no greater gift than that of gathering our family together for family prayer. They established the practice as a priority of daily living. I believe there will be few things equal to the value of doing the same for our posterity.

13

A Decree

"Prayer is not something of relative insignificance that we may choose to do if the fancy strikes us. Rather, it is an eternal decree of Deity. 'Thou shalt repent and call upon God in the name of the Son forevermore' was his first word in this dispensation. . . . Prayer opens the door to peace in this life and eternal life in the world to come. Prayer is essential to salvation. Unless and until we make it a living part of us so that we speak to our Father and have his voice answer, by the power of his Spirit, we are yet in our sins." (Bruce R. McConkie, "Why the Lord Ordained Prayer," *Ensign*, Jan. 1976, 9)

Our lives function around laws, rules, and decrees. We understand that we should stop when we see a red light or a stop sign. In the United States we have come to pay attention to April fifteenth each year as the day we must be compliant to income tax regulations, or we know we can be penalized. We generally don't question the natural law of gravity, knowing that if we were to walk off the edge of a cliff or skyscraper, we would fall downward through the air until we hit something solid to stop or deflect us. I bear large and noticeable waxlike scars on the palms of each of my hands as a result of violating the laws associated with a hot, burning coal stove. The list can go on and on. Laws, decrees, rules, orders, edicts, ordinances, and commandments all carry the same meaning.

The Lord uses specific wording, giving special emphasis, in how we should respond to certain directives. Sometimes He says, "I say unto you," and other times he says, "behold" (or look, pay attention, and so on). But when He wants to let us know that there is no room for private interpretation, He uses the words "thou shalt . . ."

He says, "thou shalt not kill" or "thou shalt not steal" or "thou shalt not covet." Extra emphasis in the words helps us to understand that these things aren't just suggestions. They are clearly directives: "Do not do that!" In some cases He makes it clear what must be done. Some of those are "thou shalt make a diligent search" or "thou shalt devote all thy service" or "thou shalt love they wife with all thy heart."

As Elder McConkie reminds us, prayer is a specific commandment. The natural man is an enemy to God, so we must learn and change from our prideful tendencies. The Lord says, "change your natural tendencies to forget me" and "pray." Repent and pray. Being connected to our Father in Heaven through His Son Jesus Christ is a commandment. Left to ourselves, it is natural for us to gravitate to selfishness and stop calling upon the name of the Lord. The Jaredites are an example of this. When it was evident that God was going to confound the language of the people at the time of the Tower of Babel, Jared petitioned his brother to pray to the Lord, that they and their friends would be spared the consequence of having their language confounded. The Lord complied with the request. However, four years later they had become casual, if not completely void, of prayer in their lives. The Lord talked with the brother of Jared and "chastened him because he remembered not to call upon the name of the Lord" (Ether 2:14).

I have noticed that a person's prayer life is the first thing to go when things are going well. Apparently then, the Lord understands the necessity of a command to "repent and call upon God in the name of the son forevermore" (Moses 5:8). I don't know about you, but that's good enough for me.

Since it is a commandment and decree, the Lord always gives us attendant blessings to the things He asks of us. The benefits of repenting and praying are many. I love the words and the music to the hymn "Did You Think to Pray?" which gently reminds us of how prayer blesses us. Consider some of the lyrics: "Ere you left your room this morning, did you think to pray? In the name of Christ, our Savior, did you sue for loving favor as a shield today? Oh, how praying rests the weary! Prayer will change the night to day. So, when life gets dark and dreary, don't forget to pray" ("Did You Think to Pray," *Hymns*, no. 140).

May we be blessed by the shield of prayer—feeling the grace of God in our lives.

Prayer Self-Examination

1. How do you feel about where you are in keeping the commandment to pray? Is there a need to repent or change?

2. It seems like anything in our lives that throws us off our routine also causes us to forget things like prayer. What have you learned to do to keep prayer in your life, regardless of life's interruptions and schedule-breakers?

3. Have you shared your positive prayer experiences with anyone close to you? A child, spouse, sibling, grandparent, friend, student, or teacher? Do it today. You will both be blessed.

Scriptures for Consideration and Marking

Moses 5:8	2 Nephi 26:15
Psalm 5:3, 12	Alma 26:22
Mark 11:24–25	

A Parting Thought

I have a testimony of prayer. When I make it a part of my daily life, I am focused on the things that matter most. I have experienced clarity in my decisions and confidence to move with purpose. If prayer practice has becomes perfunctory and hasty, we don't experience the benefit the Lord intended. Therefore, I also have a testimony that when I allow prayer to slip into a casual ritual without much thought, I live without the advantages attendant to a careful prayer life. As the Lord gives us "thou shalts" and we comply, we are blessed.

14

Public Prayers

"It is not necessary to offer long and tedious prayers, either at opening or closing. It is not only not pleasing to the Lord for us to use excess of words, but it is also not pleasing to the Latter-day Saints. Two minutes will open any kind of meeting and a half minute will close it. . . . Offer short prayers, and avoid vain repetitions." (Francis M. Lyman, *Improvement Era*, April 1947, 245)

Our public prayer life begins as early as we enter a worship service. Little children are taught to close their eyes and fold their arms when a prayer is being offered. When entering nursery in Primary, we begin the process of learning how to pray in public. The custom continues until the last public benediction is given at their funeral. Public prayers are a part of our religious life and gospel culture. Therefore, it is good to be reminded occasionally what is appropriate.

In The Church of Jesus Christ of Latter-day Saints (with the exception of the sacrament prayers), we don't recite memorized orations, nor do we read prepared devotions, as in many other religions and denominations. Our practice is to offer prayers from the heart. Often when we learn how to pray in Primary, we are given help by an adult. In order to keep the prayer simple and to expedite the prayer to meet the short attention span of children, a common set of words and petitions begins to be used. Sometimes it is years before we replace them with our own heartfelt words. How many times have we heard, "Bless us to go home in peace and safety"? My own wonderful Primary teacher Sister Nelson taught us the phrase "please bless the counselors, leaders, and missionaries of the church." I can repeat, and sometimes do, that phrase without thinking.

Let's consider a few reminders regarding our public prayers. As Elder Lyman said back in the twentieth century, "our prayers should not be long and tedious." I love his counsel: "Two minutes will open any kind of meeting and a half minute will close it. . . . Offer short prayers, and avoid vain repetitions." We should learn to pray as directed by the Spirit: brief and simple prayers.

We should learn to express respect using special language of prayer. Elder Dallin H. Oaks counseled,

> The words we use in speaking to someone can identify the nature of our relationship to that person. They can also remind speaker and listener of the responsibilities they owe one another in that relationship. The form of address can also serve as a mark of respect or affection. . . . So it is with the language of prayer . . . when

we address our Heavenly Father, we should put aside our working words and clothe our prayers in a special language of reverence and respect. ("The Language of Prayer," *Ensign*, May 1993)

We should use the words *thee*, *thou*, *thy*, and *thine* versus *you* and *yours*.

We should refrain from using the same words and phrases, or vain repetitions. Wise parents and teachers of youth will do them a great service by teaching them to pray from the heart and to use their own words, adorned in the language of prayer.

Public prayers can make a difference and contribute to the spirit of meetings and classes if they are given from the heart and in the language of prayer. Ezra Taft Benson taught, "Our prayers should be meaningful and pertinent. Do not use the same phrases at each prayer. Each of us would become disturbed if a friend said the same words to us each day, treated the conversation as a chore, and could hardly wait to finish in order to turn on the TV and forget us" (Ezra Taft Benson, *God, Family, Country* [Salt Lake City: Deseret Book, 1974], 121–22).

Literary excellence in our public prayer life or wordy, flowery speech is not the goal. The objective is to help us be more sensitive to the Spirit. We should avoid being anything like the Zoramites who prayed "to be heard of men and to be praised for their wisdom." We can feel the Spirit with simple, heartfelt, brief expressions in prayer language.

Prayer Self-Examination

1. Have you considered your own public prayer life? Are you accustomed to using the "language of prayer"? Is there something that you could do to improve your public prayers?

2. Who is in your sphere of influence that you could quietly share insight about public prayer? What will you teach them? How will you do it to keep from being critical or pharisaic?

3. Will you pay special attention to the prayers being offered the next time you are in a meeting or class? When you hear and feel a prayer that edifies and brings the Spirit into the class or meeting, will you single out the person who gave that prayer and quietly tell them how much you appreciated their prayer and why?

Scriptures for Consideration and Marking

1 Corinthians 13:11	Matthew 6:7
Alma 31:20	3 Nephi 3:7
Alma 31:18–23	

A Parting Thought

You can tell a lot about the spiritual maturity of someone by the nature of their public prayers. However we should not make judgment or criticize one another in our public prayers but examine our own. We can teach our children or those within the scope of our influence —first by example and second by basic, loving instruction—without a spirit of faultfinding. Brief and simple expressions may include: Appreciation for the opportunity of being in a class or meeting. Words of gratitude for the speakers or teachers. A request that the minds of those in the class or congregation will be open to being taught by the Spirit. Asking Heavenly Father to bless specific individuals (by name) who are in need. Remembering any special situations in the ward or class that merit public mention. A simple plea to help those in attendance apply specific counsel given in the lesson or talks. Expressions of love and appreciation for the teacher or speakers. A reminder that all that is done or said in the meeting or class will help those in attendance come to Jesus Christ. These and any other brief words that come from the heart will bring the Spirit into the meeting. No recitation. No oration. Just short and simple sentences spoken from the heart and clothed in the language of prayer.

15

Come to Your Answer in Your Own Mind

"Armed with special understanding and training on what to expect from prayers, it has been easy for me to establish confidence in the Lord that if I will make the effort to study a problem out in my own mind and present my determined course to him for ratification, he will respond with a burning of acceptance or a stupor of thought as rejection." (L. Tom Perry, "Prayer" [Salt Lake City: Deseret Book, 1977], 55)

Speaking to Oliver Cowdery, who was confused about the process of translation of the Book of Mormon, the Lord says with some clarity, "Behold, you have not understood; you have supposed that I would give it unto you, when you took no thought save it was to ask me" (D&C 9:7). So, perhaps there is more to getting answers to our petitions than just simply asking. Part of asking Him is seeking for solutions on our own, to the end that our appeal for answers comes after we've made some effort to search on our own.

The Lord expects us to ask Him, having sought for

an answer first. It is interesting that young Joseph made a determination to go into the grove of trees near his father's farm to ask God which of all the churches was correct after months searching for the answer on his own. He visited several churches and tried to make sense of their religious views. Then he said, "My mind became somewhat partial to the Methodist sect, and I felt some desire to be united with them." His mother and several siblings had joined with the Presbyterians. It was in this state of confusion that he said, "While I was laboring under the extreme difficulties caused by the contests of these parties of religionists, I was one day reading the Epistle of James, first chapter and fifth verse, which reads: If any of you lack wisdom, let him ask of God, that giveth to all men liberally, and upbraideth not; and it shall be given him" (JS—History 1:6–12).

Perhaps we could think of it in this way. The Lord spoke to Joseph well before he took the path toward the grove. In Joseph's exertion, he received part one of his answer. He had studied over months and had come up with some "leanings" toward joining a denomination. The Lord then spoke via the words of James in the New Testament. After months of study, visiting congregations, talking to various leaders of those sects, and observing the example of several of his life heroes (his mother and older brother Hyrum)—the Lord answered through the scriptures. This put him on the path to the grove where he found part two of his answer from the Father and His beloved Son.

In Doctrine and Covenants 9, the Lord continued his counsel to Oliver Cowdery.

> But, behold, I say unto you, that you must study it out in your mind; then you must ask me if it be right, and if it is right I will cause that your bosom shall burn within you; therefore, you shall feel that it is right.—But if it be not right you shall have no such feelings, but you shall have a stupor of thought that shall cause you to forget the thing which is wrong; therefore, you cannot write that which is sacred save it be given you from me. (D&C 9:8–9)

I've received more clear answers to my prayers when they have been preceded by study and action on my part. In fact, very few of my wonderings have been given clarity without some significant "seeking" for answers—including several professional choices, where to live, and what home we were to purchase. Even the pivotal moments in my days, weeks, months, and years have come after serious reflection and study. The eternally critical choice to marry my sweetheart seemed to be an easy choice for me. Yet when I think about it, that decision came after hundreds of seminary lessons, fireside talks, observations of older siblings, not to mention a desire and worthiness to be able to feel the Holy Ghost's influence in my life. Study and seeking for answers sometime comes in compressed periods of time, and other times requires months or years.

I submit that in our quest for answers, Father in

DAVID A. CHRISTENSEN

Heaven will guide us to a determination of His will. Personal revelation comes to those on the move. Answers come to searching hearts and seeking minds.

Prayer Self-Examination

1. Is it your practice to study and seek for answers before you ask the Lord? Are you willing to take time to do it?
2. Do you ask Him where to look for answers and what efforts you can expend to assist in your search?
3. It is Father's mission and purpose to develop His children to become like Him and to have all that He has. How can His admonition to study and search by faith be important to our growth, development, and preparation to achieve our highest potential?

Scriptures for Consideration and Marking

D&C 9:7–9   D&C 8:2–3
JS—History 1:7–15   Ecclesiastes 7:25
D&C 6:22–24

A Parting Thought

It is true that Heavenly Father wants us to ask. President Boyd K. Packer once said, "No message appears in scripture more times, in more ways than 'Ask, and ye shall receive'" (in *Ensign*, Nov. 1991, 21). It is important to understand better what it means for us to ask. The dictionary defines *asking* as want to know, question, pose, petition, submit, appeal for, crave, and to process by query. All those synonyms suggest action. It has been my experience that the miracles of answers to our asking generally come when we are actively searching, seeking, and moving our feet—not when we are stalled or in a stop position.

16

Feeling and Spirit

"To be effective, prayers must not consist of words alone. Earnest prayers must have an appropriate blend of earnest feeling and spirit. It is the Spirit that not only teaches a man to pray, but also makes his heartfelt desires acceptable and conveyable. If a contrite spirit and a broken heart are united with faith unwavering, our prayers, no matter how simple the words, will be significant." (Marvin J. Ashton, "Prayer" [Salt Lake City: Deseret Book, 1977], 77)

Someone once said that "memory is the mother of feeling." When we remember past and current blessings, there comes a feeling of gratitude and appreciation. Our memories of the Lord's tender mercies—sweet manifestations of the Lord's hand in our and our loved ones' lives—and appreciation for angels on the earthly side of the veil allow us to call upon Father in gratitude and humbly request for blessings.

Read Elder Ashton's quote again. What principle does he emphasize? A broken heart and contrite spirit. What is a broken heart? How can we know if our spirit is contrite? I believe humility, meekness, remorse, repentance, and a spirit of sincerity are part of it. It also speaks of a spirit of sacrifice. The word *broken* means to be separated or injured. The word *contrite* means to be sorry, apologetic, ashamed, or regretful. So, when we go before the Lord separated from the world and injured by earthly challenges with an attitude of feeling sorry and apologetic for our natural man tendencies—combined with faith in Him and His Beloved Son—then we have an optimum interchange.

As a young teen I disobeyed my parents one Sabbath afternoon when they were inside resting. I decided to take a quick ten-minute ride on the Massey Ferguson tractor and then return it to its place in the barn. I rationalized that it was a worthy means of enjoying my new capacity to drive in God's nature—the quiet countryside surrounding our home. The short ride took me across a shallow arroyo (creek) where splashes of water saturated the foot pedal clutch and the bottom of my shoe, making the clutch a little slick. True to my sense of the passing time, I returned. I was driving the tractor a little faster than I should have down a gentle slope leading to the open barn, thinking I could apply the brakes and stop appropriately in place. As I entered the barn and attempted to engage the clutch, my foot slipped off and there was no time to recover and break. The tractor crashed through the side of the wood barn and stopped with my face less than a foot from the remaining wall. Besides the hole in the barn wall, I could have been seriously injured. As I climbed off the tractor, shaking from all that had happened so quickly, I was humbled. I knew this was a problem I couldn't simply gloss over. In a spirit of sorrow, shame, and regret, I walked to the house, quietly entered the back door, and found my dad still resting in his recliner. I apologetically approached Dad and told him about my folly. Together we returned to the barn where he surveyed the damage. Then, in a spirit of love he told me he was glad I wasn't hurt and that we'd figure out a way to rebuild the shattered barn wall.

My love for Dad and not wanting to disappoint him was important to me. That feeling became the basis for my broken heart and contrite spirit. I knew that he loved me. My humble heartfelt apology was received, and he reciprocated with kindness in discussing the solution to the problem. This feeling between father and son fostered a high level of sweet communication between us.

Love, gratitude, humility, sorrow, meekness, repentance, remorse, sacrifice, and apology—earnest feelings to bring to our prayers. With these feelings, our hearts and minds are ready to commune with our Father in Heaven in a special way. The connection yields an effective two-way prayer. Father is always ready. We, on the other hand, need to prepare ourselves and to feel fit and prepared to commune.

Prayer Self-Examination

1. How long has it been since you've sought to create the earnest feeling to really communicate with Heavenly Father—by remembering?

2. Can you think of personal experiences you've had that help you to feel and understand the nature of God and His love for us—especially when you know you've disappointed Him? If so, consider writing them down in your study or personal journal. Perhaps you could tell someone else about your feelings and experience.

3. Which of all the attributes is the hardest for you to apply? Why?

Scriptures for Consideration and Marking

D&C 20:37   Helaman 8:15

3 Nephi 9:20   D&C 21:9

3 Nephi 12:19

A Parting Thought

It is probable we will need to work on this frequently to have the kind of effective prayers of which Elder Ashton speaks. But it is worthy of our effort to make the attempt more often. I have found that remembering past experiences where I can see His tender mercies and by recognizing my faults and failings—with a sincere desire to change and become better—help this process.

17

A Means to Communicate

"No Father would send His children off to a distant, dangerous land for a lifetime of testing where Lucifer was known to roam free without first providing them with a personal power of protection. He would also supply them with means to communicate with Him from Father to child and from child to Father. Every child of our Father sent to earth is provided with the Spirit of Christ, or the Light of Christ (see D&C 84:46). We are, none of us, left here alone without hope of guidance and redemption." (Boyd K. Packer, "Prayer and Promptings," *Ensign*, Nov. 2009, 43)

Have you ever really felt isolated? Can you think of a time when you were among people, maybe even millions of people, but had a sense you were alone? Have you ever thought about Moroni's final decades on earth? There were hundred of thousands of Lamanites who did not share his religious views and who even vowed to "put to death every Nephite that [would] not deny the Christ." Moroni tells us, "I, Moroni, will not deny the Christ; wherefore, I wander whithersoever I can for the safety of mine own life" (Moroni 1:3). That choice necessitated living in a solitary and friendless state. No doubt, this was a difficult time for Moroni. Yet during this time, his relationship with God must have been strengthened and reinforced to a lifetime best. Moroni's final messages came to us at the conclusion of those solitary days. He states, "Wherefore, I write a few more things, contrary to that which I had supposed; for I had supposed not to have written any more; but I write a few more things, that perhaps they may be of worth unto my brethren, the Lamanites, in some future day, according to the will of the Lord" (Moroni 1:4).

I recall sending our son Aaron off to Brazil before the Church had approved missionaries communicating with home via email. He received his first companion—a Brazilian who spoke no English. The area he was assigned was in a coastal area of Brazil, several hours from any other missionaries. Elder Christensen was armed with "MTC Portuguese," which provided a wonderful foundation for receiving the gift of tongues in the first months of his mission. However, in the beginning weeks and for many months as a new missionary, it was extremely challenging to communicate. When he wrote to us, his letter made it to the mission office one week later. It was then mailed from Sao Paulo and we received it two weeks later. We responded within a few days and our letter slowly traveled to the mission office two weeks later and on to Elder Christensen five to six weeks after sending his original letter. This was normal for the times. And it was understood that any questions or responses would come after the fact. After his mission, Aaron reported that two important things occurred during this time. First, he became homesick and felt more alone than any other time in his life. Second, it required that he establish a relationship with Heavenly Father and develop his capacity to communicate with Him through His Son Jesus Christ. It was difficult and even heart wrenching. However, I feel it was a wonderful way to start his mission because Aaron gained a powerful relationship with Heavenly Father and His Son, Jesus Christ during that challenging isolation.

We can have comfort in knowing that we have a Heavenly Father who loves us. He has given a means whereby we, His children, can communicate with Him. His great plan of happiness requires that we have faith and a repentant desire to change from our "natural man" state. As we demonstrate a commitment to Him through baptism, we gain a great unspeakable gift of the Holy Ghost (D&C 121:26). Father in Heaven is all inclusive in His love and thoughtful of all of His children . . . all of them! He has provided the Light and Spirit of Christ for all men (see Moroni 7:16) to detect good from evil.

Yes, young Elder Christensen learned about the power of prayer and establishing a relationship with Heavenly Father through Jesus Christ. Moroni formed a solid and unbreakable tie with heaven and gave us some of his best writing and counsel in his final decades. May we all fully appreciate the "gift" God has given to all of us, His children, to form a link, a connection with the powers of heaven through prayer.

Prayer Self-Examination

1. If you have had personal seasons (days, weeks, months, or years) when you felt alone or isolated, take time to write them down in your study or personal journal. Identify what you learned about the absence of, or blessing of, prayer in your life.

2. Do you feel you are strengthening your prayer life at this time? What can you do better to fortify your connection?

3. Go back and read the quote by President Packer at the beginning of this chapter. Which phrase or concept speaks most to you? Why?

Scriptures for Consideration and Marking

Moroni 7:16–19   D&C 121:36
3 Nephi 19:22   Mosiah 4:9
D&C 88:126

A Parting Thought

I love President Packer. His messages and stories are pure, simple, and easy to understand. We have a Father who loves us. He has provided us with a perfect means to stay connected with Him. We need not ever be alone, isolated, or without assistance in this life. His only requisite is that we work at and learn to pray. May we all be blessed with a testimony of this power and gift and maintain it to the end.

18

Stay Away from the Trivial

"The Spirit of the Lord is not likely to give us revelations on matters that are trivial. I once heard a young woman in testimony meeting praise the spirituality of her husband, indicating that he submitted every question to the Lord. She told how he accompanied her shopping and would not even choose between different brands of canned vegetables without making his selection a matter of prayer. That strikes me as improper. I believe the Lord expects us to use the intelligence and experience he has given us to make these kinds of choices." (Dallin H. Oaks, "Revelation," *New Era*, Sept. 1982, 46)

The word *trivial* has many synonyms and definitions. Let's look at some of them: unimportant, trite, insignificant, inconsequential, minor, of no account, of no consequence, of no importance, incidental, petty, small, inconsiderable, negligible, paltry, trifling, shallow, superficial, and foolish.

To a seven-year-old, it may feel like a life-and-death matter to find a lost toy. To an adolescent teen, having a clear complexion or having the perfect dress for the upcoming dance can feel vitally important. I hesitate to verbalize what may be trivial in adult prayers. Determining what is superficial and what is not is a personal matter. The Lord has spoken more than once in phrases like "trouble me no more concerning this matter" (D&C 59:22). Once approached by a member on some trivial matter, Joseph taught, "It is a great thing to inquire at the hands of God, or to come into His presence: and we feel fearful to approach Him on subjects that are of little or no consequence" (*Teachings of the Prophet Joseph Smith*, 22).

Perhaps one way of determining whether or not something is trivial, is to ask, "Will this matter be important next week or next year?" Or "If the Savior were to come for His second coming, would this be an issue He would be concerned about or which would impact my standing with Him?" Or "If I don't ever accomplish this, will my standing with God and Christ be impacted or will I lose the companionship of the Holy Ghost?" Determining what is important and what is not becomes easier as we spiritually mature.

Elder Oaks taught the following when he said,

Of course we are not always able to judge what is trivial. If a matter appears of little or no consequence, we can proceed on the basis of our own judgment. If the choice is important for reasons unknown to us, such as the speaking invitation I mentioned earlier or even a choice between two cans of vegetables when one contains a hidden poison, the Lord will intervene and give us guidance. When a choice will make a real difference in our lives—obvious or not—and when we are living in tune with the Spirit and seeking his guidance, we can be sure we will receive the guidance we need to attain our goal. The Lord will not leave us unassisted when a choice is important to our eternal welfare. (Dallin H. Oaks, "Revelation," *New Era*, Sept. 1982, 46)

One experience early in my professional life has taught me much. I had been employed by the Church Educational System for seven years and absolutely loved it. We had become concerned with the lack of development in our oldest child (see chapter 10). Some expensive and non-traditional therapy had been helpful but our insurance provider declined to cover it. We struggled over what I thought was a critical, life-changing decision. "Should we leave our employment with the Church Educational System and find a job that would provide the income for the therapy we felt our daughter needed?

After much prayer, I talked with a wonderful mentor, Dan Workman, who served in the administration of the Church Educational System. As I explained my dilemma, he paused, leaned back in his chair, and said "David, can I share with you something I learned once from one of the Apostles?" He said, "Many times when we are faced with a fork in the road, we wonder which is the correct road to take?" Stretching his arms with one hand pointed to the right and the other pointed to the left, he said, "We worry and we wonder, but I have learned that much of the time the answer to which road I should choose—is 'yes'!" I was puzzled for a bit and then the truth sank in. He continued, "These questions will impact many things, but in the end the only real questions you need to answer is 'Will you be true to your covenants? Will you be a good husband and father? Will you hold your family home evenings? Will you pay your tithes and offerings faithfully? Will you be obedient and merit the blessing of the gift of the Holy Ghost? Will you keep the commandments? Those kinds of questions have eternal consequence and most of the rest do not."

I was taught. Many times since then, when I am faced with what seems like a critical decision—a fork in the road—I see the image of my friend leaning forward across the desk from me, with his arms outstretched and each hand pointing outward in each direction, saying, "Should I go this way or that way? The answer is often 'yes'!"

So should you buy one can of corn or the other? Yes! If you want corn, buy one of them. Bothering the Lord with the trivial is not appropriate. If the matters are important to our salvation and spiritual well-being the Lord will intervene and assist us. Sometimes He will even rescue us. Other times, since He knows all things, He might even allow us to take the road that will seem for a while to be the "wrong" choice, but if our hearts are right and our lives worthy, He consecrates every affliction for our gain.

Prayer Self-Examination

1. Consider the things you are praying for. Are there any things that could be considered "trivial"?

2. Look back in your life and identify issues and challenges in your past that seemed monumental but now are easy to see that they really weren't important at all. What does looking back teach you?

3. Can you identify any forks in the road you are praying about right now, where the answer might be "yes"?

Scriptures for Consideration and Marking

D&C 59:22	D&C 5:29
D&C 130:15	2 Nephi 2:2–4

A Parting Thought

Perhaps it would be good to add one important closing thought. While the answer to some questions can be "yes," there are other questions that both roads may be "no" or even "not now." We will discuss those in a later chapter. And many times the answer is clearly a "yes" for one option and "no" for the other. Brother Workman's qualifying counsel to me is summarized by the requirement to "be obedient and stay worthy" so that the Holy Ghost is fully operational in our lives. Then we will know, whether or not it's trivial. We will see which questions are eternally important and be given wisdom to choose the right.

19

More than a Checklist

"The trouble with most of our prayers is that we give them as if we are picking up the telephone and ordering groceries—we place our order and hang up. We need to meditate, contemplate, think of what we are praying about and then speak to the Lord as one man speaketh to another. 'Come now, and let us reason together, saith the Lord' (Isaiah 1:18) That is the invitation. Believe in the power of prayer. Prayer unlocks the powers of heaven in our behalf. You cannot make it alone. You cannot reach your full potential alone. You need the help of the Lord." (*Teachings of Gordon B. Hinckley*, 469–70)

Studies have been completed and books have been written supporting the extraordinary value of using checklists to maximize our effectiveness. It's fair to say that most people are accustomed to making lists to help them remember, organize, prioritize, and not to let the busyness of life crowd out important dates and appointments. President Hinckley notes that "the trouble with most of our prayers" is we allow this propensity for "list making" to slip into our prayer life. We either recycle the same list for every prayer—perhaps customizing our standard list and adding a few items at the end. Or maybe we create a short list of "wants and needs" and recite them as though we were making an online order, putting items in our shopping basket.

President Hinckley reminds us that the most effective prayer is a process based upon meditation (meaning contemplation, thought, pondering, reflection, concentration, and consideration). He invites us to remember that a prayer is not about efficiency but rather about talking to our Father in Heaven as one person speaks to another and as Isaiah adds "reasoning" together.

Interestingly, some of the best instruction I've received on "conversational prayer" has come from children. I remember one family home evening when we had played some games mingled with a spiritual thought and singing. At the conclusion, I called on our five-year-old son, Devin, to say the closing prayer. Devin was and still is one of the most loving, big hearted, and fun people I know. Devin began to converse with Father in Heaven: "Heavenly Father, we are really glad that we could have family home evening. We like it when we play together. We like to play games. Thank Thee for the new game we played tonight, but we didn't like it as much as the game we played the other night. Not the one with sticks but that other one with papers. Oh, but not the game in the backyard, but it was fun too. It was that other game when Candra fell down. Heavenly Father, do you remember?" The older kids were holding back laughter, while Devin carried on a wonderful conversation with Heavenly Father about the family games we played.

Our friends shared a story that might be instructive. Ben was six years old and Lisa was four. One night, well after midnight, our friends heard Lisa crying in her bedroom. The husband waited for his wife to get up and see what was wrong, and the wife was doing the same, hoping her husband would brave the night this time. As they silently waited for each other to respond, they both heard the door to Ben's room open. They heard him shuffle across the hall to investigate the reason for his little sister's trouble. Crying was quickly replaced with muffled conversation, so now both parents got up to observe a scene illuminated only by a small night-light near her bed. "I'm scared," sobbed Lisa. "I dreamed a boogeyman is gonna get me."

Ben sat silent for a moment and then responded, "Lisa, do you know what I do when I have bad dreams about the boogeyman?"

Lisa stopped her sniffles and answered "What?"

"It really, really, really, really helps!" Ben responded. "I say a prayer. Do you want me to say a prayer with you?" he asked.

Without any other invitation Lisa got out of bed and knelt down beside Ben, who began, "Heavenly Father, Lisa is scared of the boogeyman. Bless her not to be scared anymore. I told her that prayers really, really, really, really, help. So help her not to be scared anymore. In the name of Jesus Christ, amen." Lisa climbed into bed and Ben walked out of the room, bumping into Mom and Dad. "Oh, Lisa was scared of the boogeyman and we said a prayer. Everything is all right now," he said and walked back to his room.

I have heard the simple prayers of investigators such as Brother Torres, who said, "Heavenly Father, I don't know if I can be baptized yet because I've done some bad things in my life. I do want thee to know that I am changing. Oh yeah, you do know I'm changing, I guess. Yesterday I noticed I don't even want to do dumb things like I used to. I can't figure out, dear God, what is happening to me, but I am different. My wife even says I'm different. Do you know what I mean?"

There were no checklists with Devin, Ben, or Brother Torres when they prayed—just conversation. In each case, it was like they were conversing with Heavenly Father right there in the room.

I love to observe and participate where conversational reverent prayer is offered. I have watched prayers of childhood progress into mature conversational prayers. How tender it is to hear reverent prayers about blessings and tender mercies, and about how the Atonement impacted our lives during the day. Prayers without pretension discuss the things we are grateful for and ask for assistance in matters of need.

Prayer Self-Examination

1. How would you rate your prayers? Are they "checklist" or "conversational" in nature?
2. What can you do to enhance your prayer life by developing a greater capacity to visit with the Lord instead of going through routine lists of things we want, need, or are thankful for?

3. As you teach others to pray, what can you do to teach "conversational prayer" and avoid teaching a checklist process?

Scriptures for Consideration and Marking

Isaiah 1:18

Philippians 1:4

Alma 31:19

D&C 112:10

Philemon 1:4, 22

A Parting Thought

Let's close this chapter taking President Hinckley's last few words from his quote. He said, "That is the invitation. Believe in the power of prayer. Prayer unlocks the powers of heaven in our behalf. You cannot make it alone. You cannot reach your full potential alone. You need the help of the Lord." Couple this with the counsel he gave to avoid checklist, routine, and perfunctory prayers. If we do believe we need the help of Heavenly Father to make the most of our lives—if we believe prayer is a power that unlocks heaven's forces and helps us reach our full potential—then our capacity to "become" is maximized. I have a testimony that while we can do many good things on our own, our capacity to win our greatest victories over self and all the opposition Father allows to help us grow can only happen with heaven's help. I further testify that prayer is a critical key that unlocks the power and help of Heavenly Father, Jesus Christ, the Holy Ghost, and a holy host here on earth and in heaven.

20

Willing Knees

"Many men will say they have a temper, and try to so excuse themselves for actions of which they are ashamed. I will say, there is not a man in this house who has a more indomitable and unyielding temper than myself. But there is not a man in the world who cannot overcome his [anger], if he will struggle earnestly to do so. If you find [anger] coming on you, go off to some place where you cannot be heard; let none of your family see you or hear you, while it is upon you, but struggle till it leaves you; and pray for strength to overcome. . . . When the time for prayer comes, you have not the spirit of prayer upon you, and your knees are unwilling to bow, say to them, 'Knees, get down there;' make them bend, and remain there until you obtain the Spirit of the Lord." (Brigham Young, *Journal of Discourses*, 11:290)

Sometimes we may fall into an ugly trap that is difficult to escape. It is the snare of feeling either that we aren't worthy to pray or that we don't want to pray because of our bad attitude. At that point we must pray to overcome our attitude. The Lord is willing to help us chase away those vices that prevent us from forging a connection with Him.

Have you ever experienced feelings like that? Have you ever felt that your attitude or unkind feelings toward another person prevent you from feeling close to God? Perhaps we have days when our level of spirituality wanes, and it seems our status is so low that we feel dirty, ugly, and not in a mind-set to talk to Heavenly Father. Brigham Young taught on another occasion, "It matters not whether you feel like praying . . . when the time comes to pray, pray. If we do not feel like it, we should pray till we do. . . . You will find that those who wait till the Spirit bids them pray will never pray much on this earth" (Brigham Young, *Journal of Discourses*, 13:155).

When I served as a bishop, and later as a stake president, many young people confided in me that their prayer life was not good or was rocky. I noticed a pattern in these young warriors. They had in one way or another, removed, or at least loosened, their armor of righteousness. Many were feeling the effects of their battle against Satan. Some were already wounded, and a few had fallen in battle and were near death—the spiritual kind. I definitely saw a correlation between their ability to win their battles and the relationship they had established with Heavenly Father, Jesus Christ, and the Holy Ghost.

The capacity of a person (young or old) to weather the storm of sin, anger, pornography, and so on in today's world depends in great measure upon their capacity to stay connected with heaven. The acceptance of sexual relationships prior to and outside of marriage is portrayed in the media and is accepted in society. Anger or unkind feelings are among the less salacious sins, but they are just as damning because they hold us back from connecting ourselves to heaven through prayer. Dishonesty has become the norm in a world of situational ethics. In short, Lucifer's strategies include making us feel that we are not worthy to pray or distracting us from seeking to be close to Him in prayer. We absolutely need that connection.

May I share an entry from my personal journal:

Not long ago I woke up one Sabbath morning thinking about someone who had hurt my family deeply through the violation of covenants. For fifteen or twenty minutes, my mind swarmed and my attitude spiraled downward. It is my custom to write in my journal on Sunday mornings, but I couldn't write with my swarm of ill feelings. In my swarming I missed my habitual morning prayer. It was fast day and because I hadn't prayed I just felt hungry, without thinking of the purpose of my fast. I felt like I was in a fog and didn't really want to engage in any of my normal routines. About an hour before church, the phone rang. The Gospel Doctrine teacher said, "Hello, Brother Christensen, I woke up with a high fever this morning. I was wondering if you could teach the class today?" Though my hypocritic voice was kind, I started searching for an acceptable excuse. But something nudged my soul and I said, "Yes, I will be glad to." When I hung up I looked at the lesson, checked the scripture block suggested, and started to think. Nothing came!

After forty-five minutes of trying to prepare, my mind was a blank. Now I know in teaching a class, I am not the "real" teacher. Without the Holy Ghost (the real teacher), I was doomed to fail in teaching this class. Time was running short. I felt overwhelmed, heavy hearted, and irritated with family members. I had only one place to go.

Finally, I gave in! I was losing the battle and would soon lose the war. I retired to my bedroom, closed the door, and prayed for help. I acknowledged my problem and poor reactions, and asked for forgiveness. I stayed on my knees hoping for some stroke of new light. Nothing came! The Spirit had been offended and one quick prayer was not going to solve the problem! I prayed again and asked Heavenly Father to clear my mind and spirit. I asked that He allow the Holy Ghost to return.

It was time to leave for church, we loaded the car to go to the meetinghouse. I continued in an attitude of informal prayer, meekly asking the Lord to allow the Spirit to return. As the bishop conducted sacrament meeting, I still felt empty, although I could sense a forgetfulness of my anger. Through the passing of the bread and water, I continued to pray and think about the Savior.

The answer to my prayers finally came as I listened to bearing of testimonies. I felt the Spirit return. I felt blessed peace! I didn't have a lesson plan in my mind, and didn't until I stood in front of the class. The Lord answered my prayers, and we had a successful class discussion. The rest of the day was exceptional as well, including a sweet entry in my journal and a special family dinner filled with love and laughter.

To me this experience shows a principle, a process, and an echo of the teaching of Brigham Young. When we feel unworthy to pray, Lucifer wins. When we resist our urges to call upon Heavenly Father, we lose. If we give in to bad attitudes or feelings of unworthiness, we accept a defeat in battle. Let's not allow ourselves to cut out the very thing that can reconnect us. Let's win our battles by steering clear of the excuse that we aren't worthy to pray or that we aren't in the mood to do so. Let's bend our knees and pray until we begin to feel connected again.

Prayer Self-Examination

1. Consider the story above. What may have happened if I had not prayed for the Spirit to return that Sabbath day? Make a short list.

2. Think of your own experience with this principle. Identify a time when things could have been better or a time when prayer rescued you from a downward spiral. Write in your journal about your recollections.

3. Who do you know who might be struggling with a temptation to not make prayer an active principle in their lives? What can you do to teach them that prayer is a key answer to their challenges?

Scriptures for Consideration and Marking

2 Nephi 32:8–9	Mark 14:38
2 Nephi 9:39	3 Nephi 18:15
Mosiah 26:39	D&C 31:12

A Parting Thought

We must always fight back and resist any tendency not to pray. We may be unworthy because of our actions, but one thing we will never be unfit to do is to pray. As President Young taught, "When the time for prayer comes, you have not the spirit of prayer upon you, and your knees are unwilling to bow, say to them, 'Knees, get down there'; make them bend, and remain there until you obtain the Spirit of the Lord. . . . It matters not whether you feel like praying . . . when the time comes to pray, pray. If we do not feel like it, we should pray till we do" (Brigham Young, *Journal of Discourses* 11:290).

21

Heavenly Father Answers!

What a glorious blessing! For when we want to speak to God, we pray. And when we want Him to speak to us, we search the scriptures; for His words are spoken through His prophets. He will then teach us as we listen to the promptings of the Holy Spirit. (Robert D. Hales, "Holy Scriptures: The Power of God Unto Our Salvation," *Ensign*, November 2006)

Our understanding how Heavenly Father answers prayers through scriptures can revolutionize our prayer life. It will also make our scripture study more meaningful. "When we want to speak to God, we pray. And when we want Him to speak to us, we search the scriptures." This principle is easy to understand and gives both a pattern and a system for finding answers to the questions of our souls as God speaks to us through the written words of both ancient and latter-day prophets.

Look at the experience of Joseph Smith as he determined to know which of all the churches to join. He attended the various meetings of the different sects and observed their teachings. He, no doubt, heard many sermons based on scriptural text in the Bible and surely spent time considering the various viewpoints of the clergy and religionists of the day. He said, "For the teachers of religion of the different sects understood the same passage of scripture so differently as to destroy all confidence in settling the question by an appeal to the Bible" (JS—History 1:12). Using the same Bible as a basis of conclusion, Joseph said "The Presbyterians were most decided against the Baptists and Methodists, and used all power of both reason and sophistry to prove their errors, or, at least, to make the people think they were in error. On the other hand, the Baptists and Methodists in their turn were equally zealous in endeavoring to establish their own tenants and disprove all others" (JS—History 1:9). Interpretation of biblical scripture became a part of the reason Joseph was so confused. He stated, "In the midst of this war of words and tumult of opinions, I often said to myself: What is to be done?" (JS—History 1:10).

The context of his "wonderment" and "confusion" is important as we consider the next verse. "While I was laboring under the extreme difficulties caused by the contests of these parties of religionists, I was one day reading the Epistle of James . . ." (JS—History 1:11). Confused, and seeking an answer of which church to join, Joseph read the Bible. His own record in canonized scripture does not state why he was reading the Bible. We don't know for sure whether he was seeking for a new insight to support his own partiality toward the Methodist sect, or to find reason why he should unite with them (JS—History 1:8). However we do know that he was reading the scriptures. It was in that act of faith that God spoke to his heart. He read, "If any of you lack wisdom, let him ask of God, that giveth to all men liberally, and upbraideth not; and it shall be give him" (James 1:5).

I'm not sure if the word *upbraid* was used in the everyday language of upper state New York or if it was a word regularly used in the Smith home. But if Joseph understood it at all, it would have given him confidence in the invitation to ask God. *Upbraid* means "reprimand, rebuke, admonish, chastise, chide, reprove, reproach, scold, berate, take to task, lambaste, lecture; informal—tell off, give someone a talking-to, dress down, give someone an earful, bawl out, lay into, chew out, ream out; formal—castigate."

God's promise to all who will ask Him for wisdom is that he "upbraideth not." In other words he will *not* reprimand, rebuke, scold, or turn one away. No, His answer to Joseph in that moment was clearly that He was lovingly interested in the problem Joseph was dealing with and that He would give "liberally" (or generously and unprejudiced). Receiving that answer must have been emancipating and a call to free his soul from the "war of words and tumult of opinions" he had experienced to that point.

It was not the first passage of scripture he had ever read, but it was the passage that God had given through his servant James (generally considered to be the brother of Jesus). Joseph stated, "Never did any passage of scripture come with more power to the heart of man than this did at this time to mine. It seemed to enter with great force into every feeling of my heart" (JS—History 1:12). God answered Joseph's concern of "What is to be done?" Joseph was to take another step and "ask."

When we get answers to prayers in the scriptures, we have the blessing of being able to review the answer, consider it in deeper ways, and re-read it for greater understanding. Joseph said, "I reflected on it again and again" (JS—History 1:12). What a blessing. To think and reconsider God's answers to us and find additional insight and ways in which we can act upon that answer. "Knowing that if any person needed wisdom from God, I did; for how to act I did not know, and unless I could get more wisdom than I then had, I would never know" (JS—History 1:12).

I have found in my own life that in significant moments of wonderment and war of opinions, Heavenly Father has given me important answers through His holy scriptures.

Some years ago I had been called and was preparing to serve as a mission president in South America. I was stewing over challenges in settling our family temporal affairs. My personal scripture study at that time was centered in the Doctrine and Covenants. I had been reading in Section 101, which highlights a time when the Saints in Missouri were experiencing many challenges regarding their temporal affairs. I rather lightly read over verse 16, being distracted by my own challenges. I recall finishing my scripture reading and kneeling by my chair to pray. I expressed to Heavenly Father how we had only a few weeks before we needed to have everything in order. I enumerated all the things that had to happen in that short period of time, including the sale of our home. Suddenly a thought, almost to the magnitude of a voice, came into my mind restating the scripture I had read minutes earlier. Clearly the answer came in bold and almost audible words: "Therefore, let your heart be comforted . . . be still and know that I am God" (D&C 101:16). I felt humbled, grateful, and so relieved. My thoughts and actions continued focusing on that answer in allowing the Lord, who is mindful of all things, to carry out the details regarding our call to serve. I can report that solutions to every concern were given and our preparation was complete and in place when we began our service.

I have experienced many other answers to my prayers combined with scripture reading regarding family concerns, church callings, financial affairs, and even business decisions. These answers have been given "liberally" (sometimes in interesting detail) and without upbraiding. I have been equally blessed and prepared by reading the words of our Living Prophets, Seers, and Revelators.

Prayer Self-Examination

1. Do you have regular personal scripture study?
2. Have you identified your concerns that you are

praying about in such a way that you are able to look for answers in the scriptures?

3. Do you highlight answers found in scriptural passages or write them down in a study journal that you can return and reflect on it?

Scriptures for Consideration and Marking

JS—History 1:8–12 D&C 1:38

James 1:5 D&C 18:33–36

A Parting Thought

I have a personal testimony that the Lord answers our prayers through the scriptures. I know that as we regularly read the scriptures and general conference addresses of the living oracles, we will be given answers to our prayers. We will find that Heavenly Father sharpens our judgment and decisions as we gain insight pertinent to our pleadings in prayer. My own confidence in receiving answers to prayer has been strengthened by knowing that in the omniscience of our Father in Heaven and His Son Jesus Christ, their servants have been and are inspired to make statements, give insights, and answer the problems and concerns of our prayers through the Holy Ghost and personal revelation.

22

Answers Come When We Are Serving

"Often, the answer to our prayer does not come while we're on our knees but while we're on our feet serving the Lord and serving those around us. Selfless acts of service and consecration refine our spirits, remove the scales from our spiritual eyes, and open the windows of heaven. By becoming the answer to someone's prayer, we often find the answer to our own." (Dieter F. Uchtdorf, "Waiting on the Road to Damascus," *Ensign*, May 2011)

Early in the Book of Mormon we see an example of Nephi receiving answers to his prayers and concerns as he served others. When he and his brothers failed twice to secure the brass plates from their keeper, Laban, Nephi kept trying. In these efforts, he said, "And I was led by the Spirit, not knowing before hand the things which I should do" (1 Nephi 4:6).

Another example is when Nephi and his family are in the wilderness. They found themselves in grave, and potentially life threatening, circumstances when their bows broke or lost their spring. Obtaining food seemed an impossible challenge. While the entire group, including prophet-father Lehi, grumbled and murmured in their plight, Nephi decided to try to acquire sustenance. First, with no animals in sight, he got off his knees and acted. "And it came to pass that I, Nephi, did make out of wood a bow, and out of a straight stick, an arrow; wherefore I did arm myself with a bow and an arrow, with a sling and with stones" (1 Nephi 16:23). Then he asked his murmuring father where he should go to find food.

We don't know what he thought about as he whittled, shaped the bow and arrow, and searched for a handful of perfect stones for his sling, but surely Nephi felt a great responsibility and a desire to serve those around him. He thought of his mother, sisters, brother Sam, and others in Ishmael's family, who had been supporters of the migration from Jerusalem. While serving others, Nephi used the Liahona, which provided revelatory direction. Nephi records, "I did go forth up into the top of the mountain . . . I did slay wild beasts, insomuch that I did obtain food for our families." Instead of groveling in despair, he acted in love and service to God and others, and he was given an answer.

Another example involves Nephi building a ship. After eight years in the wilderness, the families finally arrived in the land called Bountiful. Nephi received direction that was much larger and more technically difficult than whittling a bow and arrow and finding perfect stones for his sling. This time he was charged to build a

DAVID A. CHRISTENSEN

boat—a seaworthy vessel to transport this fairly large and growing group across the ocean to another hemisphere. Again, while others were mocking such an attempt or paralyzed by the impossibility of the task, Nephi moved is feet in service to the group and to a greater cause. He wrote, "The Lord did show me from time to time after what manner I should work the timbers of the ship. . . . I did build it after the manner which the Lord had shown unto me. . . . I, Nephi, did go to the mount oft unto the Lord; wherefore the Lord showed unto me great things . . . and it came to pass that after I had finished the ship according to the word of the Lord, my brethren beheld that it was good, and that the workmanship thereof was exceedingly fine" (1 Nephi 18:1–4). Nephi acted by serving and answers came.

The scriptures are full of energizing examples of individuals or groups of people acted in faith-filled service, and thus the Lord opened their eyes and gave them answers to their pleadings. Ammon and his devoted service to Lamoni literally changed the hearts and nature of a large portion of the Lamanite nation. For years Ammon and his companions acted, receiving answers to their prayers (Alma 17–26). The inspiring story of Helaman and his 2,060 stripling warriors is steeped in the attitude of service while receiving answers during a drama of changing circumstances in war (Alma 56–58). King Benjamin's example of leadership through service while receiving key doctrinal answers to his prayers is extraordinary (Mosiah 2–4).

The Doctrine and Covenants itself is a testament that the Lord answered the prayers of Joseph and early Church leaders about how to organize the restored Church of Jesus Christ. As early leaders acted by serving God and each other, their actions were directed and sometimes "movement" was corrected by divine insight.

My own experience with receiving answers to my prayers while serving others, gives additional testimony to President Kimball's words:

> I have learned that it is by serving that we learn how to serve. When we are engaged in the service of our fellowmen, not only do our deeds assist them, but we put our own problems in a fresher perspective. When we concern ourselves more with others, there is less time to be concerned with ourselves. In the midst of the miracle of serving, there is the promise of Jesus, that by losing ourselves, we find ourselves (See Matthew 10:39). Not only do we "find" ourselves in terms of acknowledging guidance in our lives, but the more we serve our fellowmen in appropriate ways, the more substance there is to our souls. We become more significant individuals as we serve others. We become more substantive as we serve others—indeed, it is easier to "find" ourselves because there is so much more of us to find! (Spencer W. Kimball, "Small Acts of Service" *Ensign,* Dec. 1974)

I have been blessed with many answers regarding how to climb my own mountains while serving others.

Prayer Self-Examination

1. Consider your own experience. Can you identify situations in your life when answers came to you while you were engaged in serving others? Have you recorded those in your personal journal?
2. Do you know anyone who is currently dealing with issues or challenges? How can you lose yourself from your own tests and trials by serving them?
3. Think of a family member or someone you know who might benefit from hearing your experience and testimony regarding the message of President Uchtdorf's quote. Find a time today when you can share it with them.

Scriptures for Consideration and Marking

1 Nephi 4:6	Mosiah 2:17
1 Nephi 16:23	Matthew 10:39
1 Nephi 18:1–4	

A Parting Thought

It is easy to get caught up thinking about our own problems. We can make a list of our needs and dilemmas in just a few minutes of time. Looking inward at our own deficiencies is natural. However, we've been admonished to "put off the natural man" and to "becometh a saint through the atonement of Christ the Lord, and becometh as a child, submissive, meek, humble, patient, full of love," (Mosiah 3:19). There are few better ways to find the answers to our own challenges than by acting and losing ourselves in the service of others.

23

Not My Will but Thy Will

"God sees things as they really are and as they will become. We don't! In order to tap that precious perspective during our prayers, we must rely upon the promptings of the Holy Ghost. With access to that kind of knowledge, we would then pray for what we and others should have—really have. With the Spirit prompting us, we will not ask amiss." (Neal A. Maxwell "Prayer" [Salt Lake City: Deseret Book, 1977], 45)

A fundamental doctrinal plank in the restored gospel is that God the Father, and His Son Jesus Christ, and the Holy Ghost are omniscient— all-knowing, all-wise, and all-seeing. Another cardinal revealed truth is that the goal of the Father, the Son, and the Holy Spirit is "to bring to pass the immortality and eternal life of man" (Moses 1:39). In other words, the entire mission and purpose of Heavenly Father is to ensure that all who have lived will, in fact, "live forever" and have an opportunity to have an eternal life or "Life of God." In other words, we are to be like Him.

Accepting and believing these basic truths will

facilitate a difference in what we pray for. Instead of pleading for random things we think we need or for circumstances to change, we pray for understanding and for strength. We replace our checklist of desires with heartfelt petition to our Heavenly Father, in the name of Jesus Christ, to help us comprehend His will, and to appreciate how the happenings and conditions we experience play into His all-knowingness and ultimate goal to bring us to a Godly station.

We approach our Father in prayer, relying on scriptural teachings that "all things have been done in the wisdom of him who knoweth all things" (2 Nephi 2:24). We seek His will as Nephi did when he stated, "O how great the holiness of our God! For he knoweth all things and there is not anything save he knows it" (2 Nephi 2:20). Remember Lehi's words to his son Jacob; "Thou knowest the greatness of God; and he shall consecrate thine afflictions for thy gain" (2 Nephi 2:2). As we pray for comprehension of our circumstantial challenges, the Lord's words to Joseph Smith provides some comfort: "Know thou, my son, that all these things shall give thee experience, and shall be for thy good."

Elder Maxwell further states, "On our own small scale we can, as Jesus did, pray that certain 'cups' will pass from us. But we must also do as He did by saying 'Nevertheless, not as I will, but as thou wilt' (see Matthew 26:39)" (Neal A. Maxwell, "Prayer" [Salt Lake City: Deseret Book, 1977], 49).

I have learned that praying to the Heavenly Father,

means not only responding to His commandment to ask Him, but to also always remember that His perspective is complete and total, and that all things are done with purpose. He desires the greatest ultimate good for His children.

A wise parent will allow certain circumstances, which may include pain and difficulty, to teach their children important principles. I'm acquainted with a father, who after his son was cited for negligence in a minor fender bender, went to the local police to solicit assistance in creating a learning experience for his son. He petitioned the citing police officer, "You are upholding traffic laws and I thank you for that. I am raising a son, and would like you to take opportunity to visit with him. Perhaps even talk to him at the police station or take him for a ride in your vehicle to impress upon him the importance of the law and being aware of how his violation of law can impact not only his life but the lives of those around him." The officer did so. He took twenty minutes to assist that father in creating a teaching opportunity, which included an "uncomfortable moment" for a sixteen-year-old boy. A lesson was learned and an important perspective was fostered. A boy's life was enhanced.

Heavenly Father is in the business of helping His children grow. He understands that certain experiences will help them learn. In the laboratory of life, sometimes our experiences bring natural consequences, which, if our hearts are right, the Lord consecrates those results to our benefit and growth. As we pray for some consequences to be softened or removed, our omniscient Father may withhold an answer so that His child may grow.

We often note the experience of Abraham and taking Isaac to the mount with a command to sacrifice his precious son. Our omniscient Father knew the final outcome of His purpose—but Abraham had to learn something about Abraham and Isaac needed to learn something about Isaac. Each was instructed and refined by the experience. We too are in need of being taught. Therefore, when we pray to our Father in Heaven in full understanding that He "knoweth all things" and that His purpose, even His glory, is to prepare us with experience and perspective, our asking becomes more mature and our seeking more focused on His will and purpose—knowing full well that our progress is His mission and goal. The Holy Ghost's role in this process is to enlighten our understanding and to confirm His will in our hearts.

Prayer Self-Examination

1. Have you developed your faith about Heavenly Father being omniscient? What can you do to strengthen that knowledge?

2. What experiences have taught you that an all-knowing Father blessed you with experiences that ultimately taught you important lessons? Have you recorded them in your journal or shared them with others?

3. Do your prayers include the statement "Not my will, but thine"? How can knowing that Heavenly Father's mission is to bless your life with the greatest ultimate

good enhance the way you pray and the results you anticipate?

Scriptures for Consideration and Marking

2 Nephi 2:24	Matthew 26:39
2 Nephi 2:20	Genesis 22:1–18
2 Nephi 2:2	

A Parting Thought

I am grateful for the understanding that we have a Heavenly Father who loves us. Everything He gives us is calculated to bless us with growth and eventual happiness. His Son, Jesus Christ, is an extension of our Father. He not only died that we might live, but also lived to show us how to live. He is the light of the world, the great exemplar, our Savior and Redeemer. The gift of the Holy Ghost is given to those who qualify to help them see more clearly, comforting them when they are down, and testifying to their minds and hearts of the divinity of God and Christ. I love knowing this truth.

24

A Formula for a Successful Marriage and Family

"On October 7, my wife, Frances, and I will have been married forty years. Our marriage took place just to the east of us in the holy temple. He who performed the ceremony, Benjamin Bowring, counseled us: 'May I offer you newlyweds a formula which will ensure that any disagreement you may have will last no longer than one day? Every night kneel by the side of your bed. One night, Brother Monson, you offer the prayer, aloud, on bended knee. The next night you, Sister Monson, offer the prayer, aloud, on bended knee. I can then assure you that any misunderstanding that develops during the day will vanish as you pray. You simply can't pray together and retain any but the best of feelings toward one another.'

"When I was called to the Council of the Twelve just twenty-five years ago this weekend, President McKay asked me concerning my family. I related to him this guiding formula of prayer and bore witness to its validity. He sat back in his large leather chair and, with a smile, responded, 'The same formula that has worked for you has blessed the lives of my family during all the years of our marriage'." (Thomas S. Monson, "Hallmarks of a Happy Home," *Ensign*, November 1988, 2)

Something very special can happen in a marriage when a couple is committed to kneeling together in prayer on a daily basis. Let's examine three examples:

First, the process of bending our knees and bowing our heads makes us more humble. We are more ready to be instructed by the Spirit when we are kneeling and asking the Lord for help in our understanding of one another. In the kneeling position, we symbolically exhibit that we are ready to be taught and are less likely to find fault.

Second, when we take turns being mouth in our prayers as couples, we can be edified as we hear our marriage partner give thanks for our union and ask for blessings upon us as we seek to fulfill our roles. Knowing that each spouse acknowledges the divine function that each plays in the marriage is edifying and unifying.

Third, as we go to Heavenly Father to discuss our blessings, our loads are made lighter. He is mindful of us and has exhibited his tender mercies in our behalf. When we articulate our challenges as a couple and family, we can become fused together in solving those problems. It puts us on the same page and helps us feel closer in love as we encounter trials and blessings given to us. In short, praying together allows us to be equally yoked in our marriage.

You can gain many benefits from praying together in couple prayers. One benefit comes when your children observe you praying together—mother and father kneeling before the Lord.

My own parents prayed together. As I compare my memories of our growing-up years with my brothers and sisters, we all remember finding our parents kneeling together in prayer. I am the sixth of nine children. When we were teenagers, it was our family rule to be at home from our evening activities before midnight. Customarily when we came home, we went into our parents' bedroom to mother's side of the bed, leaned over and whispered in her ear that we were reporting in. We then kissed her on her cheek and told her that we loved her. I don't ever remember my parents waiting up for us, but they were keenly aware of what time it was when we reported in.

One night I arrived just at the stroke of midnight, walked down the dark hallway to Mom and Dad's bedroom to report home. As I approached their doorway, I could hear my mother's voice, and I realized they were praying. Mom was acting as voice and though I could barely hear her, I detected that she was talking to Heavenly Father about their love for each other and for having been blessed with good children. Then she began with Carole, my oldest sibling and said, "Bless Carole and Irvin as they start their family." Then she asked for a blessing upon Jan and Marv in their special circumstances of dealing with a disability stemming from Jan having polio as a teenager a decade earlier. She continued in individualized petitions for Ken and Judy, my unmarried brother Steve, and for Marvin and Alice, who were engaged to be married. Knowing that I was next, I leaned in to listen more closely to what she would say to Heavenly Father about me. She said as near as I can remember, "Bless David to be successful in his love for basketball but that he will know how to keep his priorities straight. Bless him to be proper in his dating and an example among his friends. Bless him to keep good friends. Bless him in his preparation for his mission." She continued in a similar fashion for Lynette, Maureen, and finally for five-year-old Mark.

I reported in and went to bed. The memory and feeling of that night—that couple prayer—has blessed me all my life.

My brothers and sisters each had similar experiences catching our parents on their knees praying to Father in Heaven. The silhouette image of that humble couple kneeling in prayer has helped me on many occasions. I made better choices during my teen years, and it supported me through the challenges of being in a foreign country on my mission. The mental picture of their couple prayers gave me a constant assurance that my parents loved each other and that the Lord was in their marriage. That seemingly small and simple act of having consistent couple prayer has paid big dividends in the lives of their nine children and scores of grandchildren.

Prayer Self-Examination

1. If you are married, do you pray with your spouse? What can you do to improve your prayer life in this regard?

2. What blessings have you received by praying with your

spouse? How have you seen it bless the lives of others? Write about it in your journal.

3. In your prayers with your spouse, find ways to express your love, appreciation, and gratitude for them. Also give voice in asking Father to assist your spouse in his or her biggest challenges and responsibilities.

Scriptures for Consideration and Marking

1 Corinthians 7:3	Ephesians 5:23
Jacob 3:7	Proverbs 31:23
D&C 74:1	Proverbs 31:28
John 4:16	

A Parting Thought

I understand that many do not have a spouse to have an active "couple prayer life." Far too many, through no fault of their own, must move forward without a spouse or without a spouse who believes in prayer. To those, I invite you to customize the principles contained in this message to your circumstances. To the many who do have a spouse and will unite with them in prayer, take every opportunity to apply the principles in this message in improving and strengthening your marriage by being connected, as a couple, to the Lord. In all cases, our all-knowing Father in Heaven will bless us as we seek to do His will in this matter.

25

You Are Enough

"I felt very inadequate and unprepared. I remember praying, 'Heavenly Father, how can I serve a mission when I know so little?' As I prayed, the feeling came: 'You don't know everything, but you know enough'." (Neil L. Andersen, "You Know Enough," *Ensign,* Nov. 2008)

Many times the content of our prayer includes the notion that we are inadequate or lack the capacity to accomplish some task. We may feel overwhelmed and insufficient to be the perfect son, daughter, mom, or dad. We may sense we are deficient in our abilities to fulfill a new calling in the Church. Perhaps we have just been given an assignment in our employment that will require more of us than we believe we have to give. Financial or health burdens may come upon us, or someone we love, with which we feel inept to deal. In those moments, go to Heavenly Father and plead for support and added competence. This is a normal response and is a form of humility. However, humility and the feeling of inadequacy are not necessarily synonymous. Placing our faith in Jesus Christ and complete trust in our Father in Heaven are the antidotes for those moments when we feel less than qualified to meet some impending challenge.

The story of Mahonri Moriancumer (the brother of Jared) has always inspired me. He was overwhelmed with the assignment to build the Jaredite barges but managed to complete the task with strict obedience "according to the instructions of the Lord" (Ether 2:16–18). With the sea vessels completed, Mahonri asked the Lord two questions. He told the Creator of all things that the barges were well constructed, but he did not know how there would be sufficient air to breathe and light to navigate the vessels. The Lord gave him simple instructions regarding the matter of oxygen. To the matter of light, the Lord declared that He Himself would be the Master Navigator for the voyage and that in His all-knowingness it would be impossible to craft windows (due to the nature of monstrous waves and challenging seas).

Mahonri accepted the Lord's answers but knew they needed light during the passage to the Promised Land. So he went to work. He went to the mount Shelem and found ore. He created a smelter, complete with billows and everything necessary to smelt the ore. Through a great deal of energy and effort, he created sixteen small stones. Yet he knew that the stones were still simply 'stones' and nothing more. He went to the Lord and said,

> Behold, O Lord, thou hast smitten us because of our iniquity, and hast driven us forth, and for these many years we have been in the wilderness; nevertheless, thou hast been merciful unto us. O Lord, look upon me in pity, and turn away thine anger from this thy people, and suffer not that they shall go forth across this raging deep in darkness; but behold these things which I have molten out of the rock.

In other words, he pleaded, "Here are my doings—I have done all I know how to do." Mahonri then petitioned in complete faith, "And I know, O Lord, that thou hast all power, and can do whatsoever thou wilt for the benefit of man; therefore touch these stones, O Lord, with thy finger, and prepare them that they may shine forth in darkness; and they shall shine forth unto us in the vessels which we have prepared, that we may have light while we shall cross the sea" (Ether 3:3–4).

He was asking—as we must—the Lord to touch his doings and make them enough. Then the record states, "Behold, the Lord stretched forth his hand and touched the stones one by one with his finger" (Ether 3:6).

On more than one occasion the Lord took a few loaves of bread and a few fishes and fed thousands. In Matthew, two accounts show the Savior teaching and reteaching this important principle. Let's look at this account in Matthew 14:

> And when it was evening, his disciples came to him, saying, This is a desert place, and the time is now past;

send the multitude away, that they may go into the villages, and buy themselves victuals. But Jesus said unto them, They need not depart; give ye them to eat. And they say unto him, We have here but five loaves, and two fishes. He said, Bring them hither to me. And he commanded the multitude to sit down on the grass, and took the five loaves, and the two fishes, and looking up to heaven, he blessed, and brake, and gave the loaves to *his* disciples, and the disciples to the multitude. And they did all eat, and were filled: and they took up of the fragments that remained twelve baskets full. And they that had eaten were about five thousand men, beside women and children. (Matthew 14:15–21)

After all they witnessed in the feeding of the five thousand, in a different time and place, the same disciples questioned the Savior again that the food they had to offer was not enough. Again the Lord took what they had and touched it and made it enough. Look at these verses in Matthew 15:

Then Jesus called his disciples unto him, and said, I have compassion on the multitude, because they continue with me now three days, and have nothing to eat: and I will not send them away fasting, lest they faint in the way. And his disciples say unto him, Whence should we have so much bread in the wilderness, as to fill so great a multitude? And Jesus saith unto them, How many loaves have ye? And they said, Seven, and a few little fishes. And he commanded the multitude to sit down on the ground. And he took the seven loaves and the fishes, and gave thanks, and brake them, and gave to his disciples, and the disciples to the multitude. And they did all eat, and were filled: and they took up of the broken *meat* that was left seven baskets full. (Matthew 15:32–37)

The Lord can take our doings and make them enough. If He can touch sixteen small clear stones or a few loaves of bread or not many fishes and make them enough, then He can take the best we can do and make them sufficient. He can touch the sometimes frazzled mother of three preschoolers doing the best she knows how to be enough for her children. He can touch the doings of a starving student to be enough in his goal to finish school, work part time, date, save for an engagement ring, marry, and begin a family. He can touch the doings of an overwhelmed disciple with a new calling or with a daunting professional assignment. "You don't know everything, but you know enough." In other words, "You do your part and I will make you enough."

Prayer Self-Examination

1. Have you ever felt unprepared or that you lacked capability to accomplish something and then were made equal to your challenge? Have you recorded your experience(s) in your journal?

2. Who do you know that may be feeling overwhelmed? When have you felt the Lord making you equal to a challenge? What did you learn from this experience?

How can you help them to have faith and trust in the Lord?

3. Perhaps you feel inadequate in some present undertaking. Are you doing all you can while asking Heavenly Father to touch your efforts and make them enough?

Scriptures for Consideration and Marking

Ether 2:16–18	Matthew 14:15–21
Ether 3:3–6	Matthew 15: 32–37

A Parting Thought

When we have faith in the Lord Jesus Christ and trust in our Heavenly Father, their grace is sufficient to make us enough. We may not feel prepared to meet the challenges of this life. We may come up short in many things . . . but we are enough to do the will of God. I have a testimony of that truth.

26

Can One Do Evil with a Prayer on His Lips?

"We pray for wisdom, for judgment, for understanding. We pray for protection in dangerous places, for strength in moments of temptation. We remember loved ones and friends. We utter momentary prayers in word or thought, aloud or in deepest silence. We always have a prayer in our hearts that we may do well in the activities of our day. Can one do evil when honest prayers are in his heart and on his lips?" (*Teachings of Presidents of the Church: Spencer W. Kimball*, (2006), 46–58)

Several major neuroscientific studies conducted in recent years studied the concept of multitasking. We often describe our attempts as human beings to be productive by engaging in more than one thing at a time as multitasking. The term did not exist in the precomputer era. In computer terms, it describes the ability of dual or multi-processors to allow different components to engage and simultaneously perform independent tasks. However, humans don't have multi-processors. Conscious thought in human beings doesn't allow us to productively do two things at once.

While this idea can be debated, it is actually good news. Yes, we can chew gum and walk at the same time. We can do activities that do not require conscious thought while we engage in activities that do require us to think. Certainly we can justify our capacity to do more than one thing at a time.

Let's assume, at least to some degree, those who believe the notion that multitasking is a myth, are actually right. How would that theory impact us spiritually in light of President Kimball's teaching?

- Can one do evil when honest prayers are in his heart and on his lips?
- Can a person engage in praying to Father in Heaven, and look at pornography at the same time?
- Is it possible for a person to be mentally and spiritually connected to the Lord while cheating on a test at school or intentionally embezzling from an employer?
- Is it likely that an individual can address Heavenly Father in heartfelt prayer while breaking the law of chastity?
- Is it probable that a person can be petitioning Heavenly Father in the name of Jesus Christ to give them the power to keep the commandments while they succumb to drinking alcohol or smoking marijuana?

Like the debate over how effective a human being can multitask, many argue that a person can sin while praying. However, as we digest President Kimball's teaching, it helps us to understand why the Lord has counseled that we "pray always" (D&C 20:33).

He states, "We pray for wisdom, for judgment, for understanding. We pray for protection in dangerous places, for strength in moments of temptation. We remember loved ones and friends." In other words, we have our minds and hearts tilted toward God, recognizing that He can make a difference in the outcomes of our actions and even in what other people do.

He continues, "We utter momentary prayers in word or thought, aloud or in deepest silence. We always have a prayer in our hearts that we may do well in the activities of our day." Here President Kimball suggests that prayers can be formal on our knees or informal as we are about the walk and talk of our daily lives.

An outstanding missionary in Chile once shared with me that before his mission he had struggled with controlling his thoughts. He said, "President, I have never made any serious mistakes with regards to the law of chastity, but I was challenged by the Savior's admonition when he said, 'But I say unto you, that whosoever looketh on a woman, to lust after her, hath committed adultery already in his heart' (3 Nephi 12:28)." As he walked in the halls of his high school, he had a difficult time keeping his mind and imagination in check. He indicated that his eyes wandered inappropriately at nearly every girl who passed him. As we visited, he indicated that he had been successful in overcoming the challenge. He shared, "I found great power in the Lord's solution to most any problem like mine. To pray always!" He then shared with me a few of his favorite scriptures where the Lord counseled us to have a living prayer with us always.

"Therefore, let the church take heed and pray always, lest they fall into temptation" (D&C 20:33).

"Pray always, lest you enter into temptation and lose your reward" (D&C 31:12).

"Search diligently, pray always, and be believing, and all things shall work together for your good, if ye walk uprightly and remember the covenant wherewith ye have covenanted one with another" (D&C 90:24).

"Wherefore also we pray always for you, that our God would count you worthy of this calling, and fulfill all the good pleasure of his goodness, and the work of faith with power" (2 Thessalonians 1:11).

"Verily, verily, I say unto you, ye must watch and pray always, lest ye be tempted by the devil, and ye be led away captive by him" (3 Nephi 18:15)

"Pray always, that you may come off conqueror; yea, that you may conquer Satan, and that you may escape the hands of the servants of Satan that do uphold his work" (D&C 10:5).

My missionary friend had learned that when he was in an attitude of prayer, his walking dialogue went something like "Heavenly Father, here she comes. Help me to keep my eyes where they should be. Bless me to keep my thoughts pure." Or "Heavenly Father, I'm going to look at this next girl right in the eyes and say 'hello' and think of her as my sister. I ask thee to help me." Or he even said that he would pray to pretend that his mother was walking by his side or have an image of her in his mind. He would pray, "Heavenly Father, help me not to think of anything that would offend my mother." Each time he was successful, he would offer a quick prayer of gratitude, saying something like "Heavenly Father, I thank thee for helping me."

President Kimball's question is excellent. "Can one do evil when honest prayers are in his heart and on his lips?" If the human mind is focused on one thing, it is difficult for it to be focused on another. As we pray always and focus upon the Lord and His will, we can't focus on the inappropriate.

Prayer Self-Examination

1. How do you do with praying always? In what ways or times can you do better?
2. What areas of your life need more constant prayers?
3. What blessings have you received by praying always? Who can your share your experience with? Have you written your experiences in your journal?

Scriptures for Consideration and Marking

2 Thessalonians 1:11	D&C 20:33
3 Nephi 18:15	D&C 31:12
D&C 10:5	D&C 90:24

A Parting Thought

The Lord's prescription for maintaining a strong link or connection with Him is found in His admonition to pray always. When individuals have a habit of frequent informal prayers in addition to heartfelt and focused 'formal prayers', the overall quality of their prayer life is strong. The stronger the prayer life or connection with heaven, the stronger the relationship with God. The better our relationship with Heavenly Father, the less likely we are to make short-sighted choices or do things we'll regret.

27

Gratitude: A Key to Prayer

"The most meaningful and spiritual prayers I have experienced contained many expressions of thanks and few, if any, requests. As I am blessed now to pray with apostles and prophets, I find among these modern-day leaders of the Savior's Church the same characteristics that describe Captain Moroni in the Book of Mormon: these are men whose hearts swell with thanksgiving to God for the many privileges and blessings which he bestows upon His people (see Alma 48:12). . . . As we strive to make our prayers more meaningful, we should remember that in nothing doth man offend God, or against none is his wrath kindled, save those who confess not his hand in all things, and obey not his commandments (see D&C 59:21). Let me recommend that periodically you and I offer a prayer in which we only give thanks and express gratitude. Ask for nothing; simply let our souls rejoice and strive to communicate appreciation with all the energy of our hearts." (David A. Bednar, "Pray Always" [Salt Lake City: Deseret Book, 1977], 43)

There is something extraordinarily energizing when we turn our thoughts to "thanks." Gratitude turns us away from selfish thoughts and acknowledges the goodness of Heavenly Father's hand in our lives. When we ponder in an attitude of gratitude, we are more apt to notice that God truly is in the details of our lives. A spirit of thankfulness invigorates our feelings for others, and we appreciate their contribution in our lives. We see the world through new lenses when we acknowledge how all experiences, both joyful and challenging, contribute to—not take away—from our lives.

Some examples of thankful thoughts: the warm sun; the beauty of a winter snowscape; or the sweet feeling of forgiveness after a disagreement; being able to count blessings during a season of financial turmoil. When we have thankful thoughts about the tiniest flower, the glisten of the sun on icicle crystals, the sounds of leaves in the morning breeze, or a star-filled night sky, we sense a connection to our Heavenly Father.

For many years I have been inspired by these words of Elder Neal A. Maxwell:

> Small minds forget large blessings. Proud minds ceaselessly inquire of God—"What have you done for me lately?" If one is without the faith that remembers, past benefactions are forgotten because of present deprivations. For the meek and faithful, miracles—including blessings large and small, add to their gratitude and wonder. As we pray in an attitude of complete discipleship, we are swallowed up in gratitude for what He has already given. (Neal A. Maxwell, *Men and Women of Christ* [Salt Lake City: Bookcraft, 1991], 90)

Occasionally we take the opportunity in prayer to not ask Heavenly Father for anything, but rather to offer prayers of thankfulness. Sometimes it is difficult, because we generally focus more on asking for blessings. Prayers of gratitude require us to focus on our blessings and not on our deprivations or perceived needs. It has been interesting to sense what happens to our hearts when we simply contemplate those things for which we are thankful.

In applying this principle, a student once told me, "The more I prayed in a spirit of gratitude, the more I was overcome by Heavenly Father's goodness to me. I considered that, although I had been challenged by many things in my life, I was truly blessed. My parents had divorced while I was on my mission, which was one of the most difficult things I'd ever experienced. Yet, as I prayed in gratitude, I was able to see that my mother had been supported in her trial and was responding faithfully. I had experienced attitudinal challenges with one of my companions for a few months, yet I was able to see how, during that period of my service, I had personally grown in testimony and capacity. As I dedicated myself to enumerating my blessings, there came a point when I felt that I would be amiss to ask for even one thing from Heavenly Father. Because of my long list of blessings, I knew that Heavenly Father knew me and I felt a desire to be a better person and to resist being a begging disciple."

An attitude of gratitude in our prayer life is a key

to our connection with heaven. We will be less selfish and prideful as we remember our blessings. Our capacity to lift others will be greater as we "count our many blessings."

Consider some of the lyrics of a favorite hymn:

When upon life's billows you are tempest-tossed, when you are discouraged, thinking all is lost, count your many blessings; name them one by one, and it will surprise you what the Lord has done. . .

When you look at others with their lands and gold, think that Christ has promised you his wealth untold. Count your many blessings; money cannot buy your reward in heaven nor your home on high. (*Hymns*, no. 241)

Prayer Self-Examination

1. In what ways are you living with an attitude of gratitude? How have your prayers included expressions of thankfulness?

2. Consider making a tangible list (or creating one in your journal) of the blessings you've received. Take that list with you from time to time as you pray and consult with Heavenly Father in prayer.

3. Find a time to tell a friend or family member about the blessings you've received and testify of Heavenly Father's love for all his children.

Scriptures for Consideration and Marking

Alma 48:12	Romans 1:21
D&C 59:21	Jacob 4:3
D&C 78:19	D&C 62:7
Colossians 3:15	Mosiah 7:12
Psalm 100:4	

A Parting Thought

I wholeheartedly recommend Elder Bednar's counsel to us all: "Let me recommend that periodically you and I offer a prayer in which we only give thanks and express gratitude. Ask for nothing; simply let our souls rejoice and strive to communicate appreciation with all the energy of our hearts" (David A. Bednar, "Pray Always" [Salt Lake City: Deseret Book, 1977], 43). That practice will deepen our relationship with Heavenly Father and also energize us to be more faithful in our discipleship. Counting blessings great and small clears our minds and enhances our ability to see the hand of God in our lives.

28

"Yes" and "No" Are Answers, but So Is "Grow"!

"He [Heavenly Father] is our perfect Father. He loves us beyond our capacity to understand. He knows what is best for us. He sees the end from the beginning. He wants us to act to gain needed experience: When He answers yes, it is to give us confidence.

"When He answers no, it is to prevent error. When He withholds an answer, it is to have us grow through faith in Him, obedience to His commandments, and a willingness to act on truth." (Richard G. Scott, "Learning How to Recognize Answers to Prayer," *Ensign*, Nov. 1989)

Have you ever wished you could ask a simple question and get a simple answer? Looking back to my youth, I applaud my wonderful parents for their wisdom and good judgment in raising nine children. As a child, I would ask my parents if I could go to a friend's house to play. The answer was a simple yes or no. When I asked, "Can I go to a friend's house for a sleepover?" I knew the answer before I asked the question. It was always no! Sometimes I whined and presented a case for why it was unfair, but the answer was still no, and there was no question about it. Sometimes I asked, "Dad, can we go swimming in the river this afternoon?" Often he would say, "That's a great idea— yes, let's go right after you gather the eggs and feed the chickens. Go tell the other boys!" The response was clear, easy to understand, and it was an answer I liked. Those were simple days. I always got an answer I could easily understand.

When I became a teenager, once in a while when I asked a question or inquired about participating in an activity, I was given a clear answer of 'yes' or 'no'. But most often, I got no answer at all. Mom or Dad would say, "Well, David, this is a decision you'll have to make on your own." They often added, "I think you know how we feel about it, but you think about it and decide." Or worst, they may say, "That seems like a good thing" and then would add, "But have you considered this other option? David, you can't do everything. Choose wisely what would be best." Often in those days, I just wanted to go back to childhood and have my parents give me a simple yes or no answer.

Perhaps they should have taken a definitive stance at times and said "NO!" But I think my parents understood they were not just making judgments between good and bad—they were raising a boy. One evening as I was leaving the house with my cousin Doug, I told my parents we were going to a dance. I didn't think they knew anything about the dance hall, the kind of music played there, or the environment. It was called the "Green Door" and was a popular place for teens and young adults to gather for dancing and socializing. It was the late sixties when marijuana was just hitting the scene and the hippie movement was just getting underway. Alcohol, as in every era, was a challenge for many youth and monitoring it at the Green Door was loose. While Doug and I knew the reputation of the place, our inactive friend was in the band. We justified that we'd go just to support him. Maybe our attention would help him return to church, we reasoned. Dad said, "Well, David, I haven't heard great things about the Green Door. Have you thought this through?" I justified our motives about helping our friend. Dad was quiet for a minute and then said, "Well, I'm not going to tell you what to do. You are old enough to decide, but I would ask you a personal favor." I was pleased. Dad had put me on my own and had seemingly given his blessing to proceed. Then he said, "If you've decided to go, then I guess you'll be going. But do me a favor. Take just three to four minutes while you are there and look around—just look at those who are there, and what everyone is doing, and ask yourself if that's what you want to be."

I left the house and got into the car with Doug. We were pleased to have permission to go to the Green Door. We arrived, paid our rather expensive entrance fee, and entered a smoke-filled hall. Some people were dancing, while others gathered around a stage where the rock band was playing loud and heavy music. We saw our friend, who was playing lead guitar and singing lyrics we couldn't understand. We saw another acquaintance or two who were a little surprised, I think, to see us there—knowing we were Mormons and not generally in that environment. As we walked the perimeter of the dance floor to see who else we might know, one of our friends approached us drunk, smelling of alcohol. A couple sat wrapped around each other, embracing while listening to the music. Other than three or four acquaintances, this was new crowd to me. Then I remembered Dad's invitation: "Do me a favor and take just three to four minutes while you are there and look around—just look at those who are there and what everyone is doing, and ask yourself if that's what you want to be."

In that instant, I looked at Doug and he looked at me. I said, "Let's get out of here!" to which he replied before I was even finished, "I was just going to say the same thing." We left after no more than five minutes, forfeiting the hard earned dollars we'd paid for entrance. That was truly an important moment for both Doug and me.

Dad could have given a yes or a definitive no answer. However, my great father instinctively understood that my growth was the objective. Part of his reason for withholding an answer was to demonstrate his trust in my ability to see what I needed to see. His response had a purpose and a reason. My personal growth mattered. The experience I gained that night helped me in future decisions. I gained an important desire to be more obedient and less inclined to wander into anything that might have even the appearance of evil. I gained more faith in my earthly father, as well as my Father in Heaven. I felt a greater desire to stay away from the edge. That experience blessed my life.

Elder Scott reminds us that Father in Heaven has purpose and reason in withholding answers as well. "When He withholds an answer, it is to have us grow through faith in Him, obedience to His commandments, and a willingness to act on truth." We will do well to remember Him and to wisely use the agency given to us.

Prayer Self-Examination

1. Is Heavenly Father withholding any answers from you at this time in your life? If so, is there any predictable reason He might have for your growth?

2. Looking back in your life, can you see experiences where, from hindsight's revelatory perspective, that you learned important lessons? Were your faith righteous desires increased by His withholding answers from you? Write about them in your journal.

3. Is there anyone you know who is struggling with receiving answers to their prayers? Perhaps you can share with them Elder Scott's quote and share your testimony and experience.

Scriptures for Consideration and Marking

D&C 121	JS—History 1:13
D&C 122:7	JS—History 1:28–29

A Parting Thought

I am grateful for the perspective that Heavenly Father, like my own earthly father, has purpose and reason for being silent and keeping simple answers from us. I have come to understand that growth is the purpose and glory of our Father in Heaven in every regard. To grow we must gain more faith in Him and His Son. We must understand that obedience is the first law of heaven if we are to obtain the full blessings Heavenly Father has for us. We must gain a greater desire to be obedient with exactness. I have a testimony that our agency is increased as we make choices that are in accordance with the truth.

29

Behold Your Little Ones

"Notice that He didn't say 'glance at them' or 'casually observe them' or 'occasionally take a look in their general direction.' He said to behold them. To me that means that we should embrace them with our eyes and with our hearts; we should see and appreciate them for who they really are: spirit children of our Heavenly Father, with divine attributes" (M. Russell Ballard, "Great Shall Be the Peace of Thy Children," *Ensign*, Apr. 1994, 59).

A child's prayer is something very special. My personal testimony of the power of prayer in a united group of children was fortified several years ago while serving as a bishop. Our ward Primary had well over a hundred children—they were wonderful.

We had a great desire to fill the hearts of the members of our ward with the spirit of missionary work. We prayed about how to best accomplish that goal. We met with the missionaries and discussed how we might proceed. However, when we concluded the meeting, we were still working in generalities. We agreed to meet later to continue our discussion and make a plan.

The next Sunday my schedule was full, as usual, with meetings and other responsibilities associated with the bishopric. My sweet wife always insisted that we eat our main family meal together on the Sabbath. As mealtime approached, the table was set and eight hungry kids waited patiently (I assumed) for me to come home from my meetings. When I arrived, we gathered around the table and each one knelt by their chair for our customary family prayer preceding the meal. They had waited long enough for mealtime and were restless, so I made a calculated decision to call upon the one child in our family who was not long winded and would offer a concentrated family prayer—my ten-year-old son—the perfect choice for the occasion. I said, "Aaron, would you please offer our family prayer and blessing on the food?" A quick "Sure, Dad!" preceded a short pause before he launched into his signature quick and all inclusive prayer. Then he stopped short. I was curious enough that I discreetly opened one eye to see if he was okay. When I did so, other family members were peeking as well. Aaron was thinking about something. Then he continued as the rest of us closed our eyes to listen again—as this was not his traditional style. He said, "Heavenly Father, bless us as a family to have missionary experiences daily, bless the doors and hearts of our nonmember neighbors to be open to learning about the Church." He paused again and then blurted out, "And bless our ward to have baptisms monthly." I confess, I peeked again and thought, This is a good boy. He continued on at full speed and ten seconds later he said, "Amen." All the children jumped up, and we began to eat. That meal was delicious that day. I felt so happy about my extraordinary son.

The following morning at breakfast, we again knelt to have family prayer around the kitchen table. I called upon one of our daughters, Aaron's younger sister, Chalonn, who was by nature much more deliberate and complete in her prayers (like her mother). She accepted the invitation and began, "Heavenly Father, we thank thee for our blessings and our family. Please bless us as a family to have missionary experiences daily. Bless the doors and hearts of our nonmember neighbors to be open to learning about the Church, and bless our ward to have baptisms monthly." I peeked again. I thought to myself "Wow, two great missionary-minded kids." Breakfast tasted even better that day too. I was impressed with my children.

What I did not know was that several children in my ward were praying in similar ways in their family and personal prayers. The missionaries had visited the Primary on Sunday and had asked if the children wanted to help them. Everyone responded with an enthusiastic yes and the missionaries taught them a simple prayer. "Heavenly Father, we thank thee for our blessings and our family. Please bless us as a family to have missionary experiences daily, bless the doors and hearts of our nonmember neighbors to be open to learning about the Church, and bless our ward to have baptisms monthly."

Do you know what happened in fairly short order?

Heavenly Father blessed many people in our ward to have missionary experiences daily. The doors and hearts of our nonmember neighbors began to be open to learning about the Church. And, yes, our ward began to have baptisms monthly. The prayers of the children transformed the missionary life of our ward.

Prayer Self-Examination

1. Have you seen power in the prayers of children in your life? If so, write down those experiences in your journal. Let them inspire you.
2. Have you underestimated the power of a child's prayer in your own family? Perhaps you can invite them to pray about specific things.
3. What can you do to teach this and other principles of prayer to others? Do it.

Scriptures for Consideration and Marking

Matthew 18:4	Mosiah 3:19
Matthew 10:15	3 Nephi 11:37–38
Mark 10:15	3 Nephi 9:22
Luke 18:16–17	Proverbs 22:6

A Parting Thought

Children possess many admirable attributes that the Lord esteems as important enough to invite us all to become like them. King Benjamin in the Book of Mormon specifically noted the important attributes of children in his teachings. He said in order to be spiritually fit we must put "off the natural man and becometh a saint through the atonement of Christ the Lord, and becometh as a child, submissive, meek, humble, patient, full of love, willing to submit to all things which the Lord seeth fit to inflict upon him, even as a child doth submit to his father."

I hope to become more childlike.

30

The Song of the Righteous

"In addition to blessing us as Church and family members, the hymns can greatly benefit us as individuals. Hymns can lift our spirits, give us courage, and move us to righteous action. They can fill our souls with heavenly thoughts and bring us a spirit of peace.

"Hymns can also help us understand the temptations of the adversary. We encourage you to memorize your favorite hymns and study the scriptures that relate to them. Then, if unworthy thoughts enter your mind, sing a hymn to yourself, crowding out the evil with good. . . .

"Know that the song of the righteous is a prayer unto our Father in Heaven, 'and it shall be answered with a blessing upon [your] heads'." (The First Presidency, *Hymns of the Church of Jesus Christ of Latter-day Saints*, x)

I would be remiss in writing about prayer's power if I did not include my testimony of the value of hymns as prayer unto our Father. The Lord himself said, "For my soul delighteth in the song of the heart; yea, the song of the righteous is a prayer unto me, and it shall be answered with a blessing upon their heads" (D&C 25:12). What a wonderful pronouncement and promise. The next verse gives a "wherefore" or, in other words, a consequently, this is what you can expect from allowing hymns to serve as special prayers. The Lord continues, "Wherefore, lift up thy heart and rejoice, and cleave unto the covenants which thou hast made." Cleaving or being loyal to our commitments to the Lord demonstrates a faithfulness that will bind the Lord to deliver on His promises to us (D&C 25:13).

I have a strong testimony of the value of the hymns in connecting us with heaven. I have a vivid memory when I was a high school junior, of a significant strengthening of my testimony that Heavenly Father loved me and that I truly was His child. That strong assurance came to the heart of this sixteen-year-old when I heard sixty children in our ward sing "I Am a Child of God" in the annual Primary program during sacrament meeting. Something happened to my heart as those children sang like a chorus of angels. I am confident the feelings that came to me that day were in direct answer to someone else's prayers on my behalf. Perhaps it was due to the petitions of my parents, a seminary teacher, my bishop, or someone on the other side of the veil who had vested interest in my growth and love for the Lord. While I was receiving an answer to the prayers of others, I have no doubt that for some child or teacher in that Primary chorus, that same hymn was their prayer to God. They communed with Heavenly Father in song while the Lord simultaneously spoke to my heart and lifted my understanding.

I am a child of God, and he has sent me here, has given me an earthly home with parents kind and dear. Lead me, guide me, walk beside me, help me find the way. Teach me all that I must do to live with him someday. (Children's Songbook, 2)

I shall never forget that answer to my teenage heart and the connection I felt to heaven's power. I knew no temptations were worth disappointing my Father in Heaven.

I know a man who, as a former bishop, had many times provided assistance to those challenged with financial setbacks. After serving as bishop, he had a major economic challenge and professional catastrophe himself. One late night after praying with his sweetheart, he lay in bed wondering how he would provide food for his wife and growing family and how he would deal with the probability of losing their home. The phone rang. It was a dear friend with whom he had served in the Church. "Hello, I am calling from my cell phone. I am in your driveway, and I want you to come out and help me. I ask that you not speak to me or say anything—just come and help me. Okay?" Following the instructions he went out to the dark driveway and his friend handed him a box of canned goods and said, "Here, help me move this into your house." His vehicle was loaded to capacity with food. Quietly they worked together to move the boxes into the house. No words were spoken between either of them until they were finished. Then the friend handed him an envelope with a sizeable amount of cash in it and said, "You are loved by God and by lots of people in this area. Now, go back into the house and have a good night's sleep." Stunned, the man walked back into his home and embraced his wife, who was puzzled by the late-night commotion. He said, "I am thankful for the help, but how can I live to possibly accept this kind of handout?" Pride began to raise its ugly head. He could hardly accept the gift. His mind knew that was wrong, so he prayed for days for a change of heart.

Still struggling a few days later, three congregational hymns were sung in sacrament meeting, providing an answer to his prideful misery. These hymns soothed his aching and prideful heart. The first contained words from heaven that penetrated his core.

> Be thou humble in thy weakness, and the Lord thy God shall lead thee, shall lead thee by the hand and give thee answer to thy prayers. Be thou humble in thy pleading, and the Lord thy God shall bless thee, shall bless thee with a sweet and calm assurance that he cares. ("Be Thou Humble," *Hymns*, no. 130)

The second included an answer from heaven that reminded him that when we are given blessings of the Lord, we too must give blessings to others. When others keep that admonition to give, it naturally requires that someone else receive. Finally, the short closing hymn was a benediction to all answers that came to his heart that day. The congregation sang,

As I have loved you, love one another. This new commandment: Love one another. By this shall men know ye are my disciples, If ye have love one to another. ("Love One Another," *Hymns*, no. 308)

The Lord states, "The song of the righteous is a prayer unto me, and it shall be answered with a blessing upon their heads. Wherefore, lift up thy heart and rejoice, and cleave unto the covenants which thou hast made" (D&C 25:12–13).

Prayer Self-Examination

1. What experiences have you had where the lyrics and melody of a hymn has given you solace, an answer, or something to ponder about? Have you written about your experiences in your journal or shared it with a loved one?

2. Next time you are struggling with questions and concerns and are searching for an answer to your prayers, scan the hymnbook. The Lord may well answer your concerns through a hymn.

3. Follow the counsel of the First Presidency. Read one more time the quote at the beginning of this chapter and devise a plan to apply it.

Scriptures for Consideration and Marking

D&C 25:12–13   Psalm 33:2–4
D&C 136:28   Psalm 96:1–3
1 Chronicles 16:9

A Parting Thought

May you be blessed by the hymns. May you find answers to the prayers of your heart. May the lyrics of the hymns be your own feelings of praise and supplication to heaven. May your connection to heaven be strengthened by the power in prayer from the hymns.

31

A Benedictory Plea and Promise

"I offer a plea that each of us will seek to live closer to the Lord and to commune with Him more frequently and with increased faith.

"Fathers and mothers, pray over your children. Pray that they may be shielded from the evils of the world. . . . Husbands, pray for your wives. . . . Wives, pray for your husbands. . . . Pray for wisdom and understanding as you walk the difficult paths of your lives. I am confident you will be blessed." (Gordon B. Hinckley, "Benediction," *Ensign*, May 2003, 99–100)

With this final chapter of our study of prayer, I hope you have learned, or have been reminded, of principles of prayer that will assist you in your private quest to have a better prayer life. Prayer is one of the special blessings our Heavenly Father has given to assist us in navigating our lives here on earth. Our connection to heaven keeps us close to Heavenly Father always, in the name of Jesus Christ. Our capacity to benefit from the unspeakable gift of the Holy

Ghost is dependent, in large measure, upon this connection to Deity.

Prayer Self-Examination

1. How is your prayer life?
2. Is there anything you've done during the reading of this book that has helped you become more connected to heaven?
3. What is one thing you will do to enhance your prayer life?
4. Is there someone you could help in establishing a better connection to heaven? Share with them one principle or idea you've learned or been reminded of.
5. Read President Hinckley's quote again. What one or two things impress you most about his counsel in this benedictory chapter?

My Benedictory Parting Thought

I conclude with this thought. I am in awe of the goodness of most of Heavenly Father's children. I believe we each desire a better connection with Heavenly Father. I believe that God is mindful of us and loves each of us in a personal way. I have a testimony of the divinity of Jesus Christ as our Savior and Redeemer. Because of that testimony, I also have a testimony of the Holy Ghost in our lives. I have a very strong testimony of the teachings of the living prophets, and that it behooves each of us to fix our eyes and hearts on them and their instruction. By faith in the Lord Jesus Christ and by the Spirit's promptings, I understand the need to repent and change daily. I believe you know these things too. Good people like you comprehend the need to be obedient to the commandments, to move through life developing a sacrificial heart, and seeking to live the laws of the gospel. It is not hard to recognize that we should be clean, chaste, charitable, virtuous, and become consecrated in our attitude and behavior. In short, I believe in the goodness of Heavenly Father's children—you.

Therefore, it is my hope and prayer that as we move along the path of life, that we will be successful in making course corrections when needed. What we know is not always reflected in what we do. And no matter how good we are or how well we've done in the past, all of us can be better. We can each take steps to increase our effectiveness in our formal, informal, public, and private prayers. I love the words of this hymn. May you also be inspired by it:

> Oh, bless me when I worship thee To keep my heart in tune, That I may hear thy still, small voice, And, Lord, with thee commune. ("Oh, May My Soul Commune with Thee," *Hymns*, no. 123)

May we see clearly that all of our efforts to be good are magnified and enhanced when we maintain a connection with heaven. May we see how every other principle of the gospel—every covenant we make and keep, all that we are and will become—depends largely on how well we are connected to our Heavenly Father through prayer. May we be vigilant, consistent, and joyful in establishing and maintaining a special connection with Deity by sharpening and improving our prayer life. This is my prayer for you, myself, my family, and all of God's children.

About the Author

David A. Christensen's love for present day prophets was sparked as a young returned missionary student at Brigham Young University when he took the religion class Teachings of the Living Prophets. He has a testimony of listening to and seeking to follow those who are charged with helping us understand the Lord's will and direction in our lives. David has taught the same course, Teaching of the Living Prophets, for over two decades at BYU–I. He sought to pass on that same testimony and love for the counsel given by living prophets to missionaries he served with when he presided over the Chile Santiago North Mission, the Guatemala MTC, and in his service as stake president and bishop.

He counts his eight children and growing number of grandchildren as his most important converts, and his best friend and wife, Deena Bond Christensen, his eternal companion.

0 26575 12876 5